Scripture Is a Compass to Jesus Christ

By Stephane Miron

DORRANCE PUBLISHING CO
EST. 1920
PITTSBURGH, PENNSYLVANIA 15238

Dorrance Publishing Co
585 Alpha Drive
Suite 103
Pittsburgh, PA 15238
Visit our website at *www.dorrancebookstore.com*

ISBN: 979-8-88729-035-5
eISBN: 979-8-88729-535-0

Index

Introduction   5

1- Never Underestimate the Power of Planting a Seed   1

2- Allowed for Teaching and Correction?   5

3- The Seed Finally Took Root   11

4- Purpose of This Book   17

5- Belief Alone Is Not Enough   25

6- WHAT IS WORSHIP?   37

7- Do You Truly Love GOD?   43

8- Giving Your Life to Christ   45

9- Knowing a Tree by Its Fruits   51

10- Who Is the Holy Spirit?   53

11- What It Means to "Walk in the Spirit"   59

12- Praying in the Spirit   65

13- Praying Against the Devil and His Schemes   71

14- Put on the "Full Armor of GOD"   79

15- Speaking the Truth   87

16- What Is It that Grieves the Holy Spirit?   93

17- Understanding the Spirit of Lust   99

18- Overcoming the Spirit of Lust!   101

19- Marriage and Becoming One!   107

20- Not All Sins Are the Same, Sexual Immorality, Adultery, and Fornication!   113

21- Facing the Last Days without Fear   117

22- Conclusion of the Book   125

Introduction

Greetings brother or sister soul, I hope you enjoy the process of reading this book. As you will notice, this book is based humbly on my opinion, knowledge, and understanding I came to acquire in my journey of finding Jesus Christ. Although I give my humble opinion or point of view, I always use Scripture to guide my writing. This book is not to argue or contradict Scripture, but to share the Truth and Light which can be found within Scripture, hence the name of the book, *"Scripture is a Compass to Jesus Christ."*

Myself, like many others, grew up in a world which has distorted, twisted, and manipulated Scripture to appease those who seek to destroy the written word of GOD and the Teachings of our LORD and Savior Jesus Christ taught to us clearly in Scripture which you learn by reading and studying the Holy Bible.

I was raised in a Christian home; both of my parents were so-called Christians and believers of Jesus Christ. My mother believed in God as loving, forgiving, and understanding. My father would describe and display the traits of GOD as justice, rules and punishment, who obliged and forced us to attend church, and became enraged and physical when he deemed we were at fault. My mother, on the other hand, would not force, but guide and encourage; she would not get angry, but display patience, compassion, and love.

As a young man, I was confused; my parents seemed to have different views or representation as to who GOD is, including GOD's will and ways, based on their understanding and perception of who Jesus Christ is.

To make matters worse, every Sunday we would go to church

5

and listen to priests preach, what I like to call "happy Jesus," 'then after church, went back to their normal lives. Many churchgoers I recognized from the neighborhood, some were family, some friends, and some were fellow men and women. To be completely honest, besides a select few, most were liars, cheated, hated, gossiped, selfish behavior, greedy, arrogant, expressing ungodly behavior in their everyday lives, and so on. Yet, despite all that, they attended mass on Sundays, listened to "happy Jesus" preaching, and walk out believing they were Christians, and that GOD had forgiven them for their way of life. Beyond my comprehension, the priest would claim to bless them as they poured money in the basket, and they would leave church with the impression of accomplishment.

Now, don't get me wrong, I deeply respect the meaning of the Church as the Temple of Almighty GOD and His Son, Jesus Christ, our LORD and Savior, but to be sincere, I humbly believe the forces of darkness and deceit infiltrate all levels of society, including the church, and try to corrupt them from within; wolves in sheep's clothing, manipulating and overlooking the written Word of GOD, deceiving many into false belief, protecting pedophilia scandals, encouraging same sex marriage, homosexuality, refusing to condemn abortion. All things which stand in opposition to the will of Almighty GOD taught in Scripture in;
-1 Timothy 6:3-5

> 3 "If any man teach otherwise, and consent not to wholesome words, *even* the words of our Lord Jesus Christ, and to the doctrine which is according to godliness;
> 4 "He is proud, knowing nothing, but doting about questions and strifes of words, whereof cometh envy, strife, railings, evil surmisings
> 5 "Perverse disputings of men of corrupt minds, and destitute of the truth, supposing that gain is godliness: from such withdraw thyself."

Let me give you a few examples. Popes claiming to pray for the poor sitting on a throne of gold, wearing a crown of gold, in a city filled with riches and gold. Now, is that just me, or does that sound wrong in so many ways? What about abortion or homosexuality, encouraged by most churches and some in the Vatican who would dare challenge the Will of Almighty GOD in His own Temple? Both deemed by The LORD as murder and abomination, and still they encourage it?

Children of Light opposed by children of darkness, battling in every aspect of our lives, but, most importantly, in The Temple of Almighty GOD, meant to teach and exemplify the written Word of GOD, and to correct the world when it loses its way. I know in my heart, some are trying really hard to maintain, teach, and obey the written Will and Word of Almighty GOD. I will not mention any names I personally know, but some archbishops, priests, pastors, ministers, teachers, fellow believers, and so forth, truly stand firm on the solid foundation which is the written Word of GOD, they understand it to be true, everlasting, and use it as a guide in their everyday lives and decisions. We see this clearly taught in Scripture in; - Ephesians 5

- Imitators of God -
-Ephesians 5:1-7

    1 "Be ye therefore followers of God, as dear children;"

    2 "And walk in love, as Christ also hath loved us, and hath given himself for us an offering and a sacrifice to God for a sweet-smelling savour."

    3 "But fornication, and all uncleanness, or covetousness, let it not be once named among you, as becometh saints;"

    4 "Neither filthiness, nor foolish talking, nor jesting, which are not convenient: but rather giving of thanks."

    5 "For this ye know, that no whoremonger, nor unclean person, nor covetous man, who is an idolater, hath any inheritance in the kingdom of Christ and of God."

    6 "Let no man deceive you with vain words: for because of these things cometh the wrath of God upon the children of disobedience."

    7 "Be not ye therefore partakers with them."

Imitators of our LORD and Savior Jesus Christ is the way in

which a Believer and Follower must conduct oneself; in the next verses we are clearly taught how to be Children of Light, explained in; - Ephesians 5:8-14

Children of Light

8 "For ye were sometimes darkness, but now *are ye* light in the Lord: walk as children of light:"

9 "(For the fruit of the Spirit *is* in all goodness and righteousness and truth ;)

10 "Proving what is acceptable unto the Lord."

11 "And have no fellowship with the unfruitful works of darkness, but rather reprove *them*."

12 "For it is a shame even to speak of those things which are done of them in secret."

13 "But all things that are reproved are made manifest by the light: for whatsoever doth make manifest is light."

14 "Wherefore he saith, awake thou that sleepest, and arise from the dead and Christ shall give thee light."

Workers of darkness like to twist, discredit, and dissolve the written Word of GOD; wolves in sheep's clothing as taught in Scripture demonstrated in:

- Matthew 7:15 "Beware of false prophets, which come to you in sheep's clothing, but inwardly they are ravening wolves."

In my humble opinion, no need to say that the world cannot demonstrate and teach us about Jesus Christ and salvation due to the fact most of them don't know Him or obey His teachings and ways, and therefore, cannot rightfully guide you in His direction.

This is why I came to the understanding only the Written Word of GOD inscribed in Scripture can teach me rightfully who is The LORD what are His ways, what is right or wrong in the eyes of The LORD. How to conduct myself, what and whom to watch out for, always with the understanding His teachings and commandments never change, are everlasting, stand true as written, and must be followed and kept at all times.

As an example, imagine you are playing a game of chess. To overcome your opponent, you must know the rules, understand and discern the concept and objective in order to have a chance of defeating your opponent. Without such knowledge, how can you overcome your opponent? The answer is quite simple—you cannot. Try winning any challenge without knowing the rules, have no or little knowledge on the concept and objective. Sounds impossible? Well, it is.

The devil is playing chess for your soul, and believe me when I say "he knows the rules, he understands and discerns the concept, and he is working hard on his objective" which is your soul. Not only does he 'know the game, he plays dirty, and as long as you are unaware of the rules, understand and discern the concept, and are unaware of the objective, or even worse, he deceived you into believing he 'doesn't exist, and no game for your soul is going on, well, I wonder, how can you win? Do you understand the consequence of defeat?

Romans 6:23 "For the wages of sin *is* death; but the gift of God *is* eternal life through Jesus Christ our Lord."

Jesus Christ was speaking to Paul in this verse in Scripture. I beg you to observe the words Our LORD spoke in: - Acts 26:18 "To open their eyes, *and* to turn *them* from darkness to light, and *from* the power of Satan unto God, that they may receive forgiveness of sins, and inheritance among them which are sanctified by faith that is in me."

Chapter 1

Never Underestimate the Power of Planting a Seed

Growing up, I was foolish and misguided, confused by the same people who were supposed to guide me in the ways of The LORD, but very few demonstrated it with their words and actions which left me disoriented in my pursuit of The LORD.

I came to a point where I lost all belief in GOD. The preaching of priests I heard in church seemed misleading and void of power and authority; add all the scandals with priests and the Vatican, and I was left more confused than resolute. I had too many questions, and no one to answer them, or so I thought.

Even though I was giving up on The LORD and letting the devil get the best of me, I had my beloved mother, who was one of the few I saw and observed doing her best, based on her humble understanding, to walk and act in accordance to the ways of The LORD, and thank GOD she never gave up on me. Above all, Almighty GOD, the Father, never gave up on me, either. My mother wouldn't always have the words to guide me, but she never failed to express love, patience, understanding, and determination when it came to my relationship with The LORD.

To make things worse, growing up, I witnessed society move further and further away from GOD. What was once right was now wrong; good was made bad; and bad was made good. For example: marriage and divorce, faithfulness and adultery, being humble and being prideful, speaking the truth and lying, moral and immoral, generous and greedy, compassion and selfishness. Up became down, and down became up, and all this without push back from representatives of Christian faith and the churches I attended. My passion for The LORD grew cold.

At the age of nine, I saw what I believed to be a demon in the doorframe of my bedroom, which I shared with my eldest brother, who was involved in Satanism and the worship of the devil; he would always say the devil and demons would visit him in his room. I always thought he was lying until I saw him, or it, with my own eyes, and finally understood what he was experiencing.

My eldest brother was absent that night. I would usually sleep in the other room with my other brother but, for some reason, beyond comprehension, I decided to transfer my bed to my eldest brother's room, not knowing what was waiting for me.

Being young and foolish, I looked up to my two older brothers, tried to copy their actions, dressed like they dressed, and listened to the music they listened to, and both listened to heavy metal music, so being the youngest brother who wanted to be like my older brothers whom I admired, so did I, little did I know at that time the effect music can have on you and within you.

I won't mention the band I had playing in the cassette player that very night, but the music was very dark, and that's when I saw him, or it. As the door began to open, I thought it was my eldest brother coming in, but what appeared was beyond words, but I will give you a glimpse of what I encountered.

I will not discuss all the physical features of what or who I saw; I will only discuss its eyes. It, or he, had no irises or pupils; the eyes were red like burning fire, not a static red, but like active fire. I knew he, or it, was looking straight at me, even though I couldn't see its irises or pupils, due to the fact I felt it physically and to the core of my soul.

The door was opening without him, or it, touching the doorknob. As I processed what I was seeing which, I must say, was only a few seconds, I stretched out from lying in bed, wanting to stop the song I had playing on the radio. I must add, for context, the song simulated a black mass ceremony with bells and chants in the beginning of the song, but I was only nine years old back then, and was unaware of what I was actually listening to. I wanted to be like my older brothers, and this is what they listened to, so I did too. Those who listened to heavy metal in the early eighties probably know which song of which I speak

To continue the encounter: as I stretched to press the *Stop* button on the radio, inches away from the button my whole body froze; I was unable to speak, unable to move any part of my body, completely paralyzed. All I could do was watch him, or it, slowly approach me, and the smirk he, or it, had was like one who would express the feeling of "I got you," and I knew he, or it, had no good intentions for my well-being.

I felt powerless, unable to speak or move. I knew I was no match for whom, or what, was before me, but I knew Jesus Christ. I didn't know Jesus Christ as I do today, but I still knew enough to beg for His help at that very moment.

I couldn't speak with my lips, so, with the voice of my soul, "the inner voice," I cried out, " "Please, help me! Please, help me! Please, help me!" Young and foolish as I was, I forgot to say, "Please, help me, Jesus," but I know, for a fact, Jesus knew very well I was crying out to Him, and as he, or it, came to grab me, he, or it, vanished. I could move again and my speech was back. I quickly got up, closed the radio, and exited that room, never to sleep there again.

Some things were made clear to me that day: demons or devils are very real, and beyond what you might think, they are no match for our Heavenly Father and our LORD and Savior Jesus Christ. By ourselves, we are no match for them, but when Jesus Christ intervenes on our behalf, darkness trembles and flees:

James 2:19 "Thou believest that there is one God; thou doest well: the devils also believe, and tremble."

Chapter 2
Allowed for Teaching and Correction?

I humbly believe The LORD allowed me to witness this encounter as a lesson. You see, even though I was young, I was not fully aware of the meaning and impact of what I encountered.

Growing up in a society which grew cold with the Will of Almighty GOD, churches submerged in scandal after scandal, and when I would attend church, no passion for Jesus Christ was expressed, only vague repetition which left me more confused. We were all sinners, and not once did a priest make me feel bad or ashamed, and the true consequences of committing sin seemed minor and irrelevant.

At least I had my loving mother who did her best to guide me to Jesus Christ. I thank Almighty GOD for making her the stubborn, patient, caring, loving person she was. I was stubborn, but she was more stubborn.

Pastors preaching about, "Ask God for money, ask God for fortune, ask God for this, and ask God for that." A chapter in this book is dedicated to "wolves in sheep's clothing," "false teachings," as expressed in:

Matthew 24:11 "And many false prophets shall rise, and shall deceive many."

The Vatican and popes claimed to represent Jesus Christ, living in a city filled with riches and gold, and to care and pray for the poor. Something didn't align in this story. Ignorant to the full Scripture in my younger days, I knew enough to discern this could not be the way and will of GOD the Father.

Since I had not yet read the whole written word of GOD taught in Scripture, I was left with no answers. My relationship with Jesus Christ remained unclear due to the fact I was unaware who Jesus truly was. You cannot truly love GOD unless you know who He truly is.

Even though I had that encounter early in my life, I grew up following my peers in a lifestyle which seemed alright for the world, but a bitter, empty feeling on my soul. I tried to be kind in an unkind world. I became a lukewarm believer and follower of Jesus Christ. To a point, I could barely see Him or hear His voice in society. But that encounter I experienced in my younger days never left my conscience.

Although it took many years to fully sink in, I came to understand what I had encountered and the signification of what The LORD had permitted me to experience. I saw it as a warning and a lesson, and what I would do with it depended on me.

The evidence of the devil and demons was made clear to me. There was no denying what I'd experienced; it was so vivid and profound, I never forgot a single second of what I'd witnessed that day. The most important lesson I learned was: if what I saw was from hell, that meant Heaven was real, GOD the Father was real, Jesus Christ was real, and archangels and angels were real, and so was the devil, fallen angels, demons, and minions from hell.

This information I processed for many years, trying to figure out this mystery on my own, thinking I could crack the code. Churches seemed to avoid these topics. The Vatican and the popes seemed to not fit the image of Jesus Christ I had in my head. Preachers made millions and private jets preaching on how to ask GOD for riches. Education establishments slowly removed Jesus. Society went from right was now wrong, and wrong was now right; abortions full speed ahead, wars and rumors of wars.

I was disoriented. From a young age, I was looking for guidance; I wanted to find Jesus Christ in a society that didn't seem to know Him. I lived years as a lukewarm believer of Jesus Christ, GOD the Father, and the Holy Spirit of GOD, known as the Holy Trinity.

But thank Almighty GOD for the stubbornness He gave my mother; she made sure my fire and passion for Jesus never ran completely out. Every time my fire and pursuit for Jesus would get low, she would make sure it never went completely out; we should never underestimate the power of planting a seed. One day it will grow. Trust me, I know for a fact.

My mother had gifted me a (KJV) Holy Bible and, like many lukewarm Christians, I had it but never actually read it. I was too foolish to understand the importance of reading and studying the written word of GOD. I had so many questions without answers, confused on the manner in which I must conduct myself to make sure I didn't end up with the devil or demon I had witnessed firsthand.

For as long as I can remember, I always tried to remain good and kind, but it was very difficult to find deep meaning to be kind in a mostly unkind world, so I adopted the position I call "conditional kindness." Understanding very well the capabilities of my dark side within, I chose to be kind and have a positive effect on the world.

Now, let me explain what I mean by "positive effect." I will use an example, simple but profound, in my humble opinion, so here we go:

Imagine, for a second, a child drawing on a sheet of paper focused on doing the best they can. Imagination and creativity running at full capacity, they finish it, filled with hope the unknowingly lucky recipient will like their drawing. The child heads towards you and offers the drawing to you.

They say "the eyes are the window to the soul."

When the child offers or displays the drawing, their eyes are glowing with positivity. You see a glow of joy and happiness, and the reaction you choose to have carries deep impact: positive effect, or negative effect, and here is what I mean:

If you react negatively, meaning, you give a quick glance or not even look at all, say, "Go away," or "I'm busy," the glow the child has in its eyes is gone. Instead of creating positivity, you dim the light on the world, and make it a little darker.

But, on the other hand, if you react positively, meaning, you say, "Wow, what a beautiful drawing!" "Your drawing is fantastic!" "You are an amazing artist; I will display it on the wall or fridge and show every-one the beautiful drawing you created for me," paying close attention to the eyes, the glow increases. The child's positive action, "making the drawing and showing the results," and your positive reaction, "encour-agement in creativity and imagination, boost in self-esteem and confi-dence, love, and compassion" and much more, but you get the point.

Positive action or intention met with positive reaction creates pure positivity which makes the world increase in positivity, meaning a little less negative than it was due to your reactions and the way you choose to conduct yourself in the world.

Once I realized this at a young age, I knew I wanted to have a positive effect on my passage here on earth.

Despite wanting to be kind, good, and bring positivity to the world, I became lukewarm in my relationship with Jesus Christ. I was offering "conditional kindness and positivity." My morals and principles were conditional, my love was conditional, and my good deeds were conditional. Even though I was mostly kind, caring, generous, and so forth, I sometimes bent my morals and principles to fit my own agenda.

Something was missing; I felt empty inside. Despite being mostly good, I lacked meaning. My will to remain good, positive and kind had no foundation, and therefore, was weakened by every incom-ing storm I faced. I wanted to know Jesus Christ and cultivate a rela-tionship with Him, but I didn't know where to look. Societies upside down, fake teachings, scandals involving pedophilia, cover-up by our faith leaders and representatives.

Something wasn't right. I was missing part of the puzzle I had been trying to solve for so long. I was like a boat searching for land without a lighthouse to safely guide me to shore. I needed answers.

Do I give in to the world and continue this path which has left me with the feeling of emptiness? I could slowly feel the darkness of this world gradually try to extinguish the light and positivity I was try-ing to maintain and bring forth.

I needed answers; I needed meaning; I desperately needed help. On my own, being foolish and stubborn, I was slowly losing my passion for remaining kind in a mostly unkind world, as well as maintaining my morals and principles in a society lacking both. I experienced and was humbly honored to have the chance to witness the lives and actions of what I would consider "examples of true believers."

Although they probably never realized it, they gave me hope and determination. Spending time with them always made me feel better, never worse, always kind, encouraging, caring, patient, helpful, always trying to guide me in the right path. Two of my closest examples are my mother and one of my uncles. I have more examples, but these two will suffice.

They were always positive even though life was not always easy. They weren't as lukewarm as I was; unconditional was their kindness, respect, love. They had a way of life I wanted to pursue, but how?

Most people don't realize how hard it is to be positive in a seemingly mostly negative world.

One thing they had in common was they both deeply believed in Jesus Christ, they both prayed daily, attended church, but unlike all the other churchgoers I would see while in church, they would actually display and act positive in a way which was unconditional. They were also bold and unashamed to speak of the love of GOD the Father, Jesus Christ the Son, our LORD and Savior, and the Holy Spirit.

There had to be a correlation here, and my attention was brought to the Holy Bible my mother had given me years earlier. I hoped the questions I had could be answered. I thought, *"Maybe this book holds the answers I cannot seem to find anywhere else".* I had to stop being foolish and stubborn. If I was to overcome, I needed to know the rules, involved players, and the objective. By myself I was failing.

Chapter 3
The Seed Finally Took Root

The seed (gift of Holy Bible) by my loving mother had finally taken root and began to grow. I began reading scripture to my children as bedtime stories, picking it up more and more to seek answers to my questions. The more I read, the more I was captivated; the answers to all my questions were being answered I began to see meaning in being positive and good. I found hope, I found purpose, I found the One I was looking for, my LORD and Savior Jesus Christ.

I filled the emptiness I had within as I finally found the real rules, the involved players, and the objective one must reach in order to receive the gift of salvation and eternal life, by the grace, mercy and purpose of Jesus Christ clearly taught in:

John 14:6-7:
> 6 "Jesus saith unto him, I am the way, the truth, and the life: no man cometh unto the Father, but by me."
> 7 "If ye had known me, ye should have known my Father also: and from henceforth ye know him, and have seen him."

Therefore, I called the book *"Scripture Is a Compass to Jesus Christ"* without the encouragement and guidance, without perseverance and determination, without the morals and principles of a select few displayed, without the gift of the Holy Bible offered by my loving mother who always displayed unconditional love, caring, patience, encouragement, and much more, I wouldn't be writing this book or be the way I have chosen to become. All this permitted by Almighty GOD.

Alone, this world was getting the best of me. I was lukewarm and confused. I felt like something was missing. The emptiness was always present despite trying to fill it with earthly things. I was living in sin. I had three times conceived before marriage (a sin). I took my marriage vows to heart and with the understanding what I spoke in my vows was not only meant to my wife to be, but most importantly, to Almighty GOD.

Even though we had separated three years after marrying (a sin if done for any other reason than fornication), costly court hearings for custody of our three children, my beloved mother passed away in my arms, one of a few who continually encouraged my pursuit to The LORD, witnessed four of my beloved dogs pass away, and lost custody of my oldest daughter. I lost my house, lost my vehicle, lost most of my furniture, moved into a small apartment, my son and youngest daughter both stopped coming to see me even though I had a 50/50 custody court order, was involved in a truck accident which should of claimed my life, but none of my bones were broken thanks to Almighty GOD—all this and the fact I've lived with daily neuropathic pain for fourteen years now.

Something was happening. For some reason, the more I was in pursuit of knowledge and understanding of the written word of GOD, taught to us in Scripture (Holy Bible), the more trials sent wave after wave. Scripture had the answers once again. I was a lukewarm believer and follower of Jesus Christ. Taught to whoever might seek in:

- Revelation 3:15-17
> 15 "I know thy works, that thou art neither cold nor hot: I would thou wert cold or hot"
> 16 "So then because thou art lukewarm, and neither cold nor hot, I will spue thee out of my mouth."
> 17 "Because thou sayest, I am rich, and increased with goods, and have need of nothing; and knowest not that thou art wretched, and miserable, and poor, and blind, and naked:"

Sins like lying, cursing, adulterous mind and flesh, lawlessness, greed, anger, regret, vengeance, hate, envy, and pride were part of who I was.

I would call it a "white lie;" the way I conducted myself was always conditional to the situation I faced. I was lukewarm, therefore, separated from the grace and mercy of Jesus Christ, making me easy prey for the devil and his schemes.

The devil was trying very hard to stop me from seeking Jesus, but my passion and desire was on solid grounds. The seed planted many years before had roots running deep and stems which could withstand the storms. The devil wanted me ignorant of the truth inscribed in the written word of GOD, taught to whomsoever sought wisdom in Scripture.

I beg you to understand the way in which we are to conduct ourselves is quite clear. The laws and commandments are quite clear. That which is to be understood and discerned as good and evil is very clear; creation and purpose are very clear; sin is explained clearly. Path to Jesus Christ and salvation is clearly taught. Past, present, and future precisely clear. Our enemy, the devil, is clearly described, for us to be mindful of his schemes. We are taught this in: 2 Corinthians 2:11 "Lest Satan should get an advantage of us: for we are not ignorant of his devices."

Life can get dark at times; Jesus Christ is the light shining bright, guiding whomsoever seeks Him through the darkness we experience in our lives. Scripture is the compass I personally use in my daily life to remain focused and aligned on His will and ways. Not on how I would want them to be to align with my understanding, but relying on GOD the Father, and His teachings and will and understanding.

Always keep in mind the written word of Almighty GOD taught to us in Scripture is not conditional, but unconditional. You cannot pick and choose; it's all or nothing and stands true and clear always in the beginning, now, and forever.

-Blessed is He who Finds Wisdom- Proverbs 3:13-35
>13 "Happy *is* the man *that* findeth wisdom, and the
>man *that* getteth understanding."
>14 "For the merchandise of it *is* better than the merchandise of
>silver, and the gain thereof than fine gold."

15 "She *is* more precious than rubies: and all the things thou canst desire are not to be compared unto her."

16 "Length of days *is* in her right hand; *and* in her left hand riches and honour."

17 "Her ways *are* ways of pleasantness, and all her paths *are* peace."

18 "She *is* a tree of life to them that lay hold upon her: and happy *is every one* that retaineth her."

19 "The LORD by wisdom hath founded the earth; by understanding hath he established the heavens."

20 "By his knowledge the depths are broken up, and the clouds drop down the dew."

21 "My son, let not them depart from thine eyes: keep sound wisdom and discretion:"

22 "So shall they be life unto thy soul, and grace to thy neck."

23 "Then shalt thou walk in thy way safely, and thy foot shall not stumble."

24 "When thou liest down, thou shalt not be afraid: yea, thou shalt lie down, and thy sleep shall be sweet."

25 "Be not afraid of sudden fear, neither of the desolation of the wicked, when it cometh."

26 "For the LORD shall be thy confidence, and shall keep thy foot from being taken."

27 "Withhold not good from them to whom it is due, when it is in the power of thine hand to do *it.*"

28 "Say not unto thy neighbor, Go, and come again, and tomorrow I will give; when thou hast it by thee."

29 "Devise not evil against thy neighbor, seeing he dwelleth securely by thee."

30 "Strive not with a man without cause, if he have done thee no harm."

31 "Envy thou not the oppressor, and choose none of his ways."

32 "For the froward *is* abomination to the LORD: but his secret *is* with the righteous."

33 "The curse of the LORD *is* in the house of the wicked: but he blesseth the habitation of the just."
34 "Surely he scorneth the scorners: but he giveth grace unto the lowly."
35 "The wise shall inherit glory: but shame shall be the promotion of fools."

Chapter 4
Purpose of This Book

My intention for writing this book is in hope that perhaps a seed will be planted, and that one of you might seek a relationship with Jesus Christ. The world and society might be confused in the way and will of Jesus Christ our LORD and Savior, but Scripture is crystal clear and unaffected by time or human understanding. I beg you to observe and discern, to acquire wisdom and understanding in this very precious teaching we humbly are guided to pursue in our everyday lives as faithful children of Almighty GOD.

- Proverbs 3:1-12 -Trust in the Lord-

1 "My son, forget not my law; but let thine heart keep my commandments:"

2 "For length of days, and long life, and peace, shall they add to thee."

3 "Let not mercy and truth forsake thee: bind them about thy neck; write them upon the table of thine heart:"

4 "So shalt thou find favour and good understanding in the sight of God and man."

5 "Trust in the LORD with all thine heart; and lean not unto thine own understanding."

6 "In all thy ways acknowledge him, and he shall direct thy paths."

7 "Be not wise in thine own eyes: fear the LORD, and depart from evil."

8 "It shall be health to thy navel, and marrow to thy bones."
9 "Honour the LORD with thy substance, and with the first fruits of all thine increase:"
10 "So shall thy barns be filled with plenty, and thy presses shall burst out with new wine."
11 "My son, despise not the chastening of the LORD; neither be weary of his correction:"
12 "For whom the LORD loveth he correcteth; even as a father the son *in whom* he delighteth."

Scripture holds all the meaningful answers. Search and you will find; knock and the door shall be opened; listen and you will hear. If you have questions, Scripture will have the answers. If you are lukewarm, as I was, Scripture will provide guidance and correction. If you seek light in the darkness, Scripture will guide you to the Holy Trinity: GOD the Father, the Son Jesus Christ, who is our LORD and Savior, and the Holy Spirit.

Without the written word of GOD, taught to us in Scripture, I had many unanswered questions. I felt an emptiness I couldn't fill. It was very difficult to find meaning; the negative energy was slowly overcoming my will and determination to be positive in my passage here on earth. I was lacking the truth and, above all, finally realized I wasn't able to do this on my own.

If you are seeking answers, meaning, and hope, you need Scripture. If you feel an emptiness you cannot seem to fill with earthly possessions, you need the written word of GOD. Are you going through trials and tribulations? You need Jesus Christ. Are you feeling unworthy and powerless? You need to read and study Scripture to gain wisdom on the love, mercy, and grace GOD the Father Has for you, clearly expressed in Scripture.

GOD the Father loves and cares for you beyond words could express. His love is perfect, beyond human understanding, without ceasing, everlasting, perfect in all ways. This is the kind of love you will find in the Holy Bible, a loving Father offering this type of love to His faithful children. Who offered His only Beloved Son, our LORD and Savior Jesus Christ, and by His purpose, meaning, and glory, we might be washed clean of sin. Jesus Christ defeated death and Hades and now holds the key of salvation and eternal life.

-Justified by Faith - Romans 3:21-26

21 "But now the righteousness of God without the law is manifested, being witnessed by the law and the prophets;"

22 "Even the righteousness of God *which is* by faith of Jesus Christ unto all and upon all them that believe: for there is no difference:"

23 "For all have sinned, and come short of the glory of God;"

24 "Being justified freely by his grace through the redemption that is in Christ Jesus:"

25 "Whom God hath set forth *to be* a propitiation through faith in his blood, to declare his righteousness for the remission of sins that are past, through the forbearance of God;"

26 "To declare, *I say*, at this time his righteousness: that he might be just, and the justifier of him which believeth in Jesus."

Therefore, I ask: How is your relationship with Jesus Christ? Do you have a relationship with Jesus? Are you seeking Him? Are you living as a lukewarm believer, as I was? Are you looking for strength, hope, guidance, clarity, discernment, wisdom in The LORD? What about knowledge in the laws, guidance, and teachings? Are you seeking answers as to the path one must follow to live in accordance to Jesus Christ, which is the only path to salvation and eternal life? Are you seeking a path of righteousness? Do you find it difficult to see the light surrounded by the darkness of the wickedness of this world?

Scripture is the compass you need to navigate through the darkness of this world. If you are lacking for a light to help you through tribulations, are you seeking strength and wisdom to come out victorious? Are you seeking purpose and meaning? Are you unsure who Jesus Christ is? Are you seeking the truth in a world that seems to have lost its way?

Are you seeking strength in your weaknesses? Is your name in the Book of Life? Are you living in disobedience to our Heavenly Father? Are you lukewarm in your belief and walk with Jesus Christ? Are you in need of discernment, wisdom, and knowledge in how to truly be able to love Jesus and obey His teachings?

How can you love, obey, and follow Jesus Christ when you are unaware of who Jesus truly is? What Jesus taught us, for example, what is right or wrong, according to the will and ways of Jesus Christ and our Heavenly Father.

Scripture is the written Word of GOD: precise, clear, uncorrupted by men, expressed and demonstrated by the life and purpose of Jesus Christ our LORD and Savior.

Path of righteousness is straight and narrow, but the path of destruction is broad and wide, as taught in:

- Matthew 7:13-14 -The Narrow Gate-
> 13 "Enter ye in at the strait gate: for wide *is* the gate, and broad *is* the way, that leadeth to destruction, and many there be which go in thereat:"
> 14 "Because strait *is* the gate, and narrow *is* the way, which leadeth unto life, and few there be that find it."

Simply believing in Jesus Christ isn't enough clearly taught in.

- James 2:19
"Thou believest that there is one God; thou doest well: the devils also believe, and tremble."

Lukewarm won't make the roster of salvation and eternal life clearly taught in: -

Revelations 3:15-17
> 15 "I know thy works, that thou art neither cold nor hot: I would thou wert cold or hot."
> 16 "So then because thou art lukewarm, and neither cold nor hot, I will spue thee out of my mouth."
> 17 "Because thou sayest, I am rich, and increased with goods, and have need of nothing; and knowest not that thou art wretched, and miserable, and poor, and blind, and naked:"

Disobedience and unfaithfulness will exclude your name from the "Book of Life" taught to us in; - Revelations 20:12-15

> 12 "And I saw the dead, small and great, stand before God; and the books were opened: and another book was opened, which is *the book* of life: and the dead were judged out of those things which were written in the books, according to their works."
>
> 13 "And the sea gave up the dead which were in it; and death and hell delivered up the dead which were in them: and they were judged every man according to their works."
>
> 14 "And death and hell were cast into the lake of fire. This is the second death."
>
> 15 "And whosoever was not found written in the book of life was cast into the lake of fire."

Homosexuality, abortion, sexual immorality, murder, theft, liars, adulterers, blasphemers, false prophets, and so forth, everything negative, evil, wicked, wrong, dark, and bad are very clearly taught, precisely, and without doubt to be had.

What is positive, good, righteous, lawful, and required in order to be obedient, faithful, and true believers and followers of Jesus Christ is also clearly taught in Scripture. The written word of GOD holds the answer to all meaningful questions you might have. Scripture is meant to guide us, teach us, and empower us with strength and wisdom found in Jesus Christ and the power in His name and purpose and glory.

- Romans 6:18-23

> 18 "Being then made free from sin, ye became the servants of righteousness."
>
> 19 "I speak after the manner of men because of the infirmity of your flesh: for as ye have yielded your members servants to uncleanness and to iniquity unto iniquity; even so now yield your members servants to righteousness unto holiness."
>
> 20 "For when ye were the servants of sin, ye were free from righteousness."

21 "What fruit had ye then in those things whereof ye are now ashamed? for the end of those things *is* death."

22 "But now being made free from sin, and become servants to God, ye have your fruit unto holiness, and the end everlasting life."

23 "For the wages of sin *is* death; but the gift of God *is* eternal life through Jesus Christ our Lord."

Scripture gives you wisdom and knowledge to overcome the devil and the forces of darkness of this world.

Use Scripture as a moral compass to keep you on the path of righteousness. Even though you fall off the path in your moments of weakness, humble yourself before Almighty GOD in a quiet place, confess your sin to our Heavenly Father (believing He will hear, and answer your request), giving thanks for His grace and mercy in your regards, and last, but not least, "Repent." I humbly beg you to understand the importance of this teaching spoken from Jesus Christ, Himself: "Repent and sin no more." Use the written word of GOD as comfort, correction, strength, and guidance to return to the straight and narrow path which leads to Jesus Christ, salvation, and eternal life.

Once I truly understood the meaning of:

- Matthew 7:13

"Enter ye in at the strait gate: for wide *is* the gate, and broad *is* the way, that leadeth to destruction, and many there be which go in thereat," and when I humbly understood;

- John 3:18-21

18 "He that believeth on him is not condemned: but he that believeth not is condemned already, because he hath not believed in the name of the only begotten Son of God."

19"And this is the condemnation, that light is come into the world, and men loved darkness rather than light, because their deeds were evil."

20 "For every one that doeth evil hateth the light, neither cometh to the light, lest his deeds should be reproved."

21 "But he that doeth truth cometh to the light, that his deeds may be made manifest, that they are wrought in God."

I needed only to look around and realize how accurate Scripture truly is. I learned in Scripture the consequences of taking the path of wickedness and disobedience to GOD the Father, and that taking such a path leads to destruction and the lake of fire.

I also learned in Scripture taught by many, but most importantly, taught by Jesus Himself, that a path of righteousness, exemplified by Jesus Christ and by His grace and mercy and purpose conquered Hades, and held the keys to salvation and eternal life.

I knew the path was straight and narrow which led to Jesus Christ and salvation, and this was the path I was seeking. I humbly understood I needed to first find such a path of righteousness exemplified and taught by Jesus Christ and many others in Scripture.

- Matthew 7:14

"Because strait *is* the gate, and narrow *is* the way, which leadeth unto life, and few there be that find it."

Scripture taught me both paths, answered the questions I had, made clear the destination of both paths, showed me the rules, the involved players, and the objective (Jesus Christ) in order to overcome the devil and his schemes, in order to be granted salvation in the purpose of Jesus Christ, and in order to live a life of righteousness in the eyes of Almighty GOD.

All men and women fall short of the glory of GOD, taught to us in; - Romans 3:23 "For all have sinned, and come short of the glory of God;"

But a life of righteousness is required also, clearly taught in:

- Proverbs 12:28

"In the way of righteousness *is* life; and *in* the pathway *thereof there is* no death."

One last example to conclude this chapter demonstrated and taught in:

- Ephesians 5:8-21 -Children of Light-

8 "For ye were sometimes darkness, but now *are ye* light in the Lord: walk as children of light:"

9 "(For the fruit of the Spirit *is* in all goodness and righteous-ness and truth ☺ "

10 "Proving what is acceptable unto the Lord."

11 "And have no fellowship with the unfruitful works of dark-ness, but rather reprove *them*."

12 "For it is a shame even to speak of those things which are done of them in secret."

13 "But all things that are reproved are made manifest by the light: for whatsoever doth make manifest is light."

14 "Wherefore he saith, Awake thou that sleepest, and arise from the dead, and Christ shall give thee light."

15 "See then that ye walk circumspectly, not as fools, but as wise,"

16 "Redeeming the time, because the days are evil."

17 "Wherefore be ye not unwise, but understanding what the will of the Lord *is*."

18 "And be not drunk with wine, wherein is excess; but be filled with the Spirit;"

19 "Speaking to yourselves in psalms and hymns and spiritual songs, singing and making melody in your heart to the Lord;"

20 "Giving thanks always for all things unto God and the Father in the name of our Lord Jesus Christ;"

21 "Submitting yourselves one to another in the fear of God."

Chapter 5
Belief Alone Is Not Enough

As demonstrated earlier, belief alone is not enough; righteousness is also required. Baring good fruit gathers treasure in Heaven, Jesus Christ taught us by exemplifying His teachings on the manner we are to conduct ourselves in our everyday lives, in righteousness and faithfulness in the will and ways of our Heavenly Father.

If you are truly seeking the path to Jesus Christ, if you need light to guide you through the darkness, if you need courage and strength to finish the race, if you feel disoriented and lost the path, are you lukewarm, as I once was, are you "eating from fruit of the tree of knowledge of good and evil" as Adam and Eve both did?

Are you deciding based on your own understanding what is good and evil? This is, in my humble opinion, "eating from fruit of the tree of knowledge of good and evil."

-Trust in the Lord - Proverbs 3:1-12

> 1 "My son, forget not my law; but let thine heart keep my commandments:"
>
> 2 "For length of days, and long life, and peace, shall they add to thee.
>
> 3 "Let not mercy and truth forsake thee: bind them about thy neck; write them upon the table of thine heart:"
>
> 4 "So shalt thou find favour and good understanding in the sight of God and man."
>
> 5 "Trust in the LORD with all thine heart; and lean not unto thine own understanding."

25

6 "In all thy ways acknowledge him, and he shall direct thy paths."

7 "Be not wise in thine own eyes: fear the LORD, and depart from evil."

8 "It shall be health to thy navel, and marrow to thy bones."

9 "Honour the LORD with thy substance, and with the first-fruits of all thine increase:"

10 "So shall thy barns be filled with plenty, and thy presses shall burst out with new wine."

11 "My son, despise not the chastening of the LORD; neither be weary of his correction:"

12 "For whom the LORD loveth he correcteth; even as a father the son *in whom* he delighteth."

Further in the book, I demonstrate how unrighteousness, wickedness, and sin separates us from the presence of GOD The Father, reunited only by repentance and forgiveness of such ways, and by the blood and purpose of our LORD and Savior Jesus Christ, forgiven, and made clean again, body, soul, and spirit.

Once cleansed, and only then, can the Holy Spirit of GOD inhabit your body, soul, and spirit; the Holy Spirit of GOD who is holy, pure, and clean, cannot dwell in a body, soul, and spirit which is unholy and corrupted.

When Jesus forgave Mary Madeleine of her sinful and unholy and wicked ways, Jesus made it very clear to anyone truly paying attention. Jesus first forgave Mary of all her past and present wicked ways and sins she had ever committed, making her body, soul, and spirit cleansed and holy, granting her the blessing of the presence of the Holy Spirit, and grace and mercy of GOD the Father, and the blessings, protection, and power gifted to all who love His Son Jesus Christ our LORD and Savior, and obey His teachings.

But as of Mary Madeleine's future, Jesus was very clear in what was required in order to remain righteous. Jesus specifically and willingly said, "Go and sin no more," meaning exactly what it is meant to teach us in our daily lives, and the way we must conduct ourselves in our journey here on earth, enabling us to have a journey of faithfulness, righteousness, holiness, and obedience to receive the gift of salvation and eternal life.

Understanding the concept which the Holy Spirit of GOD requires us to be righteous and holy in order to dwell in us, to be cleansed of our unclean self transforms us into a clean and holy body, soul, and spirit, and in order to remain righteous and holy, you must "sin no more."

Jesus Christ took upon Himself the sins of the whole world. In Him and by His purpose, we are forgiven of sin, wickedness, ungodliness, unrighteousness, and unfaithfulness. Although I beg you to understand, such a gift is to the faithful and righteous who obey His teachings and commandments, and who bare good fruit in the eyes of The LORD, taught in:

- Matthew 7:16-20 -A Tree and its Fruit-

16 "Ye shall know them by their fruits. Do men gather grapes of thorns, or figs of thistles?"

17 "Even so every good tree bringeth forth good fruit; but a corrupt tree bringeth forth evil fruit."

18 "A good tree cannot bring forth evil fruit, neither *can* a corrupt tree bring forth good fruit."

19 "Every tree that bringeth not forth good fruit is hewn down, and cast into the fire."

20 "Wherefore by their fruits ye shall know them."

You must understand profoundly the meaning and truth found in the Holy Bible if you truly want to pursue a relationship with Jesus. You will hear His voice in the written word of GOD, discern and understand what is good and evil in the eyes of GOD the Father, expressing what you have learned so far based on your current understanding of Jesus Christ, amplifying such knowledge in your daily life.

The old version of yourself, which was unholy and unfaithful, was made clean the moment you chose to be born again.

1 Peter 1:22-25 -The Word of the Lord Stands Forever-

22 "Seeing ye have purified your souls in obeying the truth

through the Spirit unto unfeigned love of the brethren, *see
that ye* love one another with a pure heart fervently:"
23"Being born again, not of corruptible seed, but of incorrupt-
ible, by the word of God, which liveth and abideth forever."
24 "For all flesh *is* as grass, and all the glory of man as the
flower of grass. The grass withereth, and the flower thereof
falleth away:"
25 "But the word of the Lord endureth forever. And this is the
word which by the gospel is preached unto you."

Your ways must also change; your priorities must change. Your under-standing on right and wrong must also be renewed and corrected. You must go from a path in which is presumed that there are no conse-quences or reaction to your intentions and actions in the world; this is a lie whispered by the devil, deceiving you into believing you know bet-ter than Almighty GOD, and that He doesn't exist; therefore, do as you please, do whatever makes you happy.

That is so wrong and deceitful in so many ways, but I under-stand it. Scripture teaches us before the second coming of Jesus Christ, the world would be in this state of affairs, taught in:

- 2 Timothy 3:1-7 -Evil in the Last Days-
1 "This know also, that in the last days perilous times shall
come."
2 "For men shall be lovers of their own selves, covetous, boast-
ers, proud, blasphemers, disobedient to parents, unthankful,
unholy,"
3 "Without natural affection, trucebreakers, false accusers, in-
continent, fierce, despisers of those that are good,"
4 "Traitors, heady, high-minded, lovers of pleasures more than
lovers of God;"
5 "Having a form of godliness, but denying the power thereof:
from such turn away."
6 "For of this sort are they which creep into houses, and lead captive silly women laden with sins, led away with diver's lusts,"

7 "Ever learning, and never able to come to the knowledge of
the truth."

When you truly decide to live and act in accordance to what is good in
the eyes of The LORD, everything you do and say beholds a deep understanding of the knowledge that your speech, actions, and intentions
which can be found the fruits you produce and will be judged upon by
Almighty GOD, an event we will all participate.

Imagine, if you will, a tree representing your journey here on
earth; your speech, actions, and intentions produce the fruits which
manifest in your tree. Good actions produce good fruits. Evil actions
produce evil fruit, clearly taught in Scripture which I wrote about further in this book.

I chose a few examples to write about in this book. I speak only
of a tiny fraction of the knowledge and wisdom taught in the written
word of GOD, but my hope is that by reading this book, I will demonstrate to you the crucial importance in reading, studying, and be made
aware, and most importantly understanding and wisdom in what you
are taught in Scripture.

The devil will try to get you to stay away from Scripture, he
don't want us to know the truth, he knows very well if we are unrighteous or lukewarm we are disobeying Almighty GOD, which excludes us
from having our names written in the book of life, therefore including
us with the many which take the path of disobedience, which leads to
destruction, clearly taught in Scripture which I mentioned earlier.

Straight is the way and narrow is the path of righteousness
which leads to Jesus Christ our LORD and Savior, Salvation, and Eternal
Life in the Kingdom of Heaven.

Scripture defines the path one must take in order to enter the Kingdom of Heaven, Jesus Christ is the only way, taught by Jesus Himself in:

- John 14:1-7 -Jesus, the Way to the Father-
1 "Don't let your hearts be troubled. Trust in God, and trust also
in me."

2 "There is more than enough room in my Father's home. If this were not so, would I have told you that I am going to prepare a place for you?"

3 "When everything is ready, I will come and get you, so that you will always be with me where I am."

4 "And you know the way to where I am going."

5 "No, we don't know, Lord," Thomas said. "We have no idea where you are going, so how can we know the way?"

6 "Jesus told him, "I am the way, the truth, and the life. No one can come to the Father except through me."

7 "If you had really known me, you would know who my Father is. From now on, you do know him and have seen him!"

In my humble opinion, Jesus taught us He was the way, meaning the way one must conduct themselves in order to love, obey, and remain faithful in the will and ways of GOD the Father in Heaven, which He taught us by exemplifying His teachings as He walked here on earth.

Secondly, Jesus said, "I am the truth," meaning He was speaking the truth about the will and ways of GOD the Father, what is good and evil in the eyes of GOD, the truth about what the rewards and blessings of faithfulness, righteousness, and belief in Jesus will bring you. Jesus also spoke truth as to the consequences and destination of the unfaithful, unrighteous, and non-believers, including the lukewarm believers who live in disobedience or, as I like to call it, "conditional belief;" their reward and destination is clearly taught in Scripture, and stand true always.

Third, Jesus said, "I Am the life," in my humble opinion meaning if you follow the straight and narrow path to Jesus Christ, correct yourself when you deviate from the path, produce good fruit, deeply and humbly discern, and obey the teachings mentioned previously of the way, and truth in which we are meant to learn, understand, and exemplify in our everyday lives, just as Jesus Christ taught and exemplified always, without fault, positivity and truth at its finest, perfect in all His ways.

We all fall short of the glory of GOD. Only in Jesus Christ can we be gifted salvation by the blood and purpose of Jesus Christ. Jesus holds the key to the gates of Heaven; understanding and recognizing this is crucial.

None is righteous in the eyes of The LORD as demonstrated previously, but a righteous life is required if you truly love, obey, and wish to please GOD the Father. Believing is not enough, as seen earlier; all the forces of darkness recognize and believe Jesus Christ is the Son of Almighty GOD and tremble in His presence, but none of them will ever enter the Kingdom of Heaven, the Kingdom of GOD our Father, which we call "paradise."

I selected only a few subjects we are taught in Scripture, the completeness of wisdom and knowledge of the will and ways which are obedient to Almighty GOD, are found in their true and everlasting form taught to us in Scripture which is the written word of GOD, found in the Holy Bible. I prefer the (King James version) which, in my humble opinion, is the less manipulated by men and closer (in my opinion) to the actual version of Scripture of the written word of GOD which is, for some odd reason, kept from us.

False morals may seem like the product only of human ignorance to us. The roots of false morals are clearly attributed to the work of the deceiver, taught in:

- 2 Thessalonians 2:7-12

7 "For the mystery of iniquity doth already work: only he who now letteth *will let*, until he be taken out of the way."

8 "And then shall that Wicked be revealed, whom the Lord shall consume with the spirit of his mouth, and shall destroy with the brightness of his coming:"

9 "*Even him*, whose coming is after the working of Satan with all power and signs and lying wonders,"

10 "And with all deceivableness of unrighteousness in them that perish; because they received not the love of the truth, that they might be saved."

11 "And for this cause God shall send them strong delusion, that they should believe a lie:"

12 "That they all might be damned who believed not the truth, but had pleasure in unrighteousness."

According to Scripture, the fountainhead of all falsehood, all misguided world views, all false religions and philosophies and all teachers of any faith other than faith in the Gospel of Jesus Christ are instigated by the father of lies.

One day, all your lies, all your blasphemy, all your choices, all your intentions, all your actions, all your gods, all your intellect, and unfiltered wisdom will fail you. Let's examine:

- Psalms 73:3

"For I was envious at the foolish, *when* I saw the prosperity of the wicked."

If you worship things of this world, if you envy people of this world, you belong to this world, and therefore are an enemy of GOD. Clearly explained and taught in:

- Romans 8 - No Condemnation in Christ

1 "*There is* therefore now no condemnation to them which are in Christ Jesus, who walk not after the flesh, but after the Spirit."
2 "For the law of the Spirit of life in Christ Jesus hath made me free from the law of sin and death."
3 "For what the law could not do, in that it was weak through the flesh, God sending his own Son in the likeness of sinful flesh, and for sin, condemned sin in the flesh:"
4 "That the righteousness of the law might be fulfilled in us, who walk not after the flesh, but after the Spirit."
5 "For they that are after the flesh do mind the things of the flesh; but they that are after the Spirit the things of the Spirit."
6 "For to be carnally minded *is* death; but to be spiritually minded *is* life and peace."
7 "Because the carnal mind *is* enmity against God: for it is not subject to the law of God, neither indeed can be."
8 "So then they that are in the flesh cannot please God."

Control by the Spirit

9 "But ye are not in the flesh, but in the Spirit, if so be that the Spirit of God dwell in you. Now if any man have not the Spirit of Christ, he is none of his."

10 "And if Christ *be* in you, the body *is* dead because of sin; but the Spirit *is* life because of righteousness."

11 "But if the Spirit of him that raised up Jesus from the dead dwell in you, he that raised up Christ from the dead shall also quicken your mortal bodies by his Spirit that dwelleth in you."

Heirs with Christ

12 "Therefore, brethren, we are debtors, not to the flesh, to live after the flesh."

13 "For if ye live after the flesh, ye shall die: but if ye through the Spirit do mortify the deeds of the body, ye shall live."

14 "For as many as are led by the Spirit of God, they are the sons of God."

15 "For ye have not received the spirit of bondage again to fear; but ye have received the Spirit of adoption, whereby we cry, Abba, Father."

16 "The Spirit itself beareth witness with our spirit, that we are the children of God:"

17 "And if children, then heirs; heirs of God, and joint-heirs with Christ; if so be that we suffer with *him*, that we may be also glorified together."

If we observe Scripture in:

- Psalms 73:17 "Until I went into the sanctuary of God; *then* understood I their end."

Once he saw and understood the reward of the unfaithfulness and unrighteous disobedience to The LORD and the destination of all who do not seek to learn and obey His laws and commandments, he no longer envied them, but instead felt pity for them.

He no longer fancied the wicked; he no longer taught how great it was to live like they lived. But instead, from that day on, he pitied them, because he saw and knew what was waiting for them if they did not turn away from wickedness and disobedience, beg forgiveness from Jesus Christ, and pursue the path of righteousness.

I beg you to observe in Scripture detailing the story of a rich man who died, was buried, then, in hell, lifted his eyes being in torment, pleaded for mercy, faced with the consequences of the fruits he bared. Taught in; - Luke 16:19-31

The Parable of the Rich Man and Lazarus

19 "There was a certain rich man, which was clothed in purple and fine linen, and fared sumptuously every day:"

20 "And there was a certain beggar named Lazarus, which was laid at his gate, full of sores,"

21 "And desiring to be fed with the crumbs which fell from the rich man's table: moreover the dogs came and licked his sores."

22 "And it came to pass, that the beggar died, and was carried by the angels into Abraham's bosom: the rich man also died, and was buried;"

23 "And in hell he lift up his eyes, being in torments, and seeth Abraham afar off, and Lazarus in his bosom."

24 "And he cried and said, Father Abraham, have mercy on me, and send Lazarus, that he may dip the tip of his finger in water, and cool my tongue; for I am tormented in this flame."

25 "But Abraham said, Son, remember that thou in thy lifetime receivedst thy good things, and likewise Lazarus evil things: but now he is comforted, and thou art tormented."

26 "And beside all this, between us and you there is a great gulf fixed: so that they which would pass from hence to you cannot; neither can they pass to us, that *would come* from thence."

27 "Then he said, I pray thee therefore, father, that thou

wouldest send him to my father's house:"

28 "For I have five brethren; that he may testify unto them, lest they also come into this place of torment."

29 "Abraham saith unto him, They have Moses and the prophets; let them hear them."

30 "And he said, Nay, father Abraham: but if one went unto them from the dead, they will repent."

31 "And he said unto him, If they hear not Moses and the prophets, neither will they be persuaded, though one rose from the dead."

Don't you think it will be a horrible thing when all your lies, all your deception, all your trickery, all your deceit, all your foolishness, all your gods, all that nonsense fail you? You will come to your senses in the lake of fire.

You can choose to follow the world, you can choose to deny The LORD and His ways, you can choose to decide for yourself what is right and wrong, which seems to be paralleled with "eating the fruit of the tree of knowledge of good and evil."

You can pretend you know better than GOD, or even worse, that the devil convinced you GOD does not exist. You can live your life as if there are no consequences but rest assured, one day you will stand before The LORD, and you will regret your arrogance and ignorance when you realize you were wrong. Furthermore, you will try to ask for forgiveness, but you will be unable to speak. You will try to beg for mercy, but you will realize mercy is no longer an option. You will try to move, but you will be kept on your knees, paralyzed by the presence of The LORD on judgment day.

The most terrifying words a humble soul can hear are taught to us in: - Matthew 7:21-23

21 "Not every one that saith unto me, Lord, Lord, shall enter into the kingdom of heaven; but he that doeth the will of my Father which is in heaven."

22 "Many will say to me in that day, Lord, Lord, have we not

prophesied in thy name? and in thy name have cast out devils? and in thy name done many wonderful works?"

23 "And then will I profess unto them, I never knew you: depart from me, ye that work iniquity."

The final words spoken by The LORD in the hour of our judgment to all who have not built a strong relationship on solid foundation with His Son, our LORD and Savior, Jesus Christ.

Hell is no place for mankind; it wasn't meant for us taught to us in: - Matthew 25:41 "Then shall he say also unto them on the left hand, Depart from me, ye cursed, into everlasting fire, prepared for the devil and his angels."

We were created perfect in the image of Almighty GOD; the abyss was for Lucifer and the fallen angels which became Satan as fallen angel, and demons as his followers who fell with him. Maybe hell existed before the fallen were cast down, but one thing I know for certain, hell was not created for the purpose of mankind.

Satan the serpent, also known as "the devil," "the deceiver," "father of all lies," and more titles I demonstrate further in the book, deceived Adam and Eve in the Garden of Eden and brought about the fall of mankind. The perfect image GOD the Father created us in was no longer perfect but corrupted by sin and disobedience, separating us from the capability to see His face, due to the unholy and disobedient creation we had become.

Everything changed at the fall of mankind; commandments were given, interpreted by many generations of people of influence throughout history until the First Coming of Jesus Christ.

Chapter 6

What Is Worship?

You give it your precious time:

Time is a very precious currency we tend to overlook. Time is a gift Our Heavenly Father offers us to play out our journey here on earth before we reunite with Him to account for the way we chose to spend it.

When you give time to a substance, you offer it your precious gift of time which is a form of worship. At any moment, you choose who or what receives it. Now tell me, who receives your precious time?

The definition of the word "worship" in the dictionary is described as such. When used as a "noun," we find this: "ritual; veneration, homage; adoration, esteem; prayer, exaltation; idol-worship." And when used as a "verb", the word "worship" is described as: "pray, exalt, venerate, deify, idolize; honor, esteem." With this in mind, let's begin the chapter.

You make it a priority. Giving time to something or someone determines who or what is a priority at that said moment for you. Every second of every minute of every day, you are giving your time to whatever you decide to say, do, achieve, or attain. Making whatever you decide priority above all other things.

What you decide to prioritize becomes a form of worship, making it the owner of your time, focus, intention, and action you do with the precious gift of Our Heavenly Father granted to us at our conception.

You can prioritize things of the Spirit or things of the flesh. It all depends on what's guiding you. Are you trying to pursue and improve the material world? Or the Spirit world? Are you prioritizing the Kingdom of Heaven or hell? Are you seeking to glorify our Heavenly Father? Or are you glorifying Satan by pursuing things of the flesh?

In the Bible we are told in: - 1 John 2:15-17

> 15 "Love not the world, neither the things *that are* in the world. If any man love the world, the love of the Father is not in him."
>
> 16 "For all that *is* in the world, the lust of the flesh, and the lust of the eyes, and the pride of life, is not of the Father, but is of the world."
>
> 17 "And the world passeth away, and the lust thereof: but he that doeth the will of God abideth for ever."

The Bible says we must not love the world. This implies we must not lust for things of this world. Many believers today are carried on by all the trends going on in the world. They lust after riches, fame, sexual desires, positions, and attention.

I am not saying having a career or goals are bad, and you should not walk around with your eyes closed. Everyone needs to put bread on the table, feed their families, and have hobbies. But what I am trying to make you understand is you must put GOD first in everything you do. His commandments and teachings should direct our daily lives.

Is faith, hope, trust, unconditional love, caring, compassion, respect, empathy, patience, understanding, generosity, guidance, humility your priority? Or does unfaithfulness, hate, selfishness, envy, revenge, anger, disrespect, carelessness, lies, discouragement, pride fill your time, making it your priority?

-You inspire to be as which you worship-

You can see this clearly in sports, music, entertainment, culture fans. For example, you can see sport fans aspire to be their preferred player; they buy clothing with their names on it, are impressed by their every move, follow their exploits, aspire to achieve such exploits, boast of their talents, hang pictures of them on their wall, know all the names and number of the team they worship.

Music fans also buy clothing of their preferred band or musician, aspire to be like them, they practice to sound like them, they prioritize their music above all other music, they gather in public places to hear them perform, some people literally faint upon seeing their favorite musicians.

Entertainment fans are similar to the ones above; they buy products with their name on them, wear clothing similar to whomever they admire, they also aspire to be like them, follow their lifestyle, prioritize them above all other actors or comedians and so on. They also gather in theaters to see them perform.

Culture fans follow the trend of the day. Since culture is on a constant change, so are they. The Smartphone is a great example; they are never satisfied with the one they have; if the trend of the day is believed to be better, they rid themselves of their current phone and pay ridiculous sums of money just to have the new one. Vehicles are the same; folks give up their current vehicle and pay ridiculous sums of money just to drive around in the new trend of the year. You see this with shoes, gaming consoles, hairstyles, the color of clothes, and the list goes on and on and on. You see the point.

All the above examples are material worship which belongs to this world, the world you can see, touch, and smell. All these things rot, rust, and decay. Since we know the earthly possessions belong to this earth, and that the current ruler of the earth is the devil, when you choose to gather earthly treasure, you are doing so by worshiping the current earthly ruler.

For those who choose to worship and prioritize our Heavenly Father, who is the Creator of this earth, meaning he exists outside this earth we call the "Heavenly Realm" or the "Spirit World;" the world you can't see, touch, or smell. This is the world from which your soul came from. Your soul was created in the image of GOD; our body is the vehicle in which we live our earthly experience. We are spiritual beings with a soul having an earthly journey in a human body. I believe this is why The LORD said to us: "I knew you before you entered your mother's womb," meaning we knew GOD before our conception.

Those who worship The Holy Trinity (The Father, The Son, and the Holy Spirit) always seek to gather treasure in Heaven. Understanding this principle, you must recognize Heavenly Realm is a Spiritual Realm. If your focus is to attain Heavenly treasure, you must do works in the Spirit, all good things seen and unseen to the human eye, faith, love, truth, compassion, respect, empathy, forgiveness, understanding. caring, guidance, humility, humbleness, kindness; and all these things must be unconditional.

Our LORD and Savior Jesus Christ, is the *key* you need to unlock the gates to enter the Kingdom of Heaven. Jesus Christ is the truth, the way, and the life. No soul shall enter the Kingdom of Heaven, except through Him, and Him alone. We are taught this in: –

John 14:6

"Jesus saith unto him, I am the way, the truth, and the life: no man cometh unto the Father, but by me."

To worship The Holy Trinity (the Father, the Son, and the Holy Spirit), seeking to gather Heavenly treasure that belong to the world we cannot see, but is most important to anyone who seeks The Kingdom of Heaven. You must prioritize all good things which were taught to us all by Our LORD and Savior Jesus Christ. Jesus Christ must be the owner of your time which guides you earthly journey. You must live daily, inspiring to be more Christ like. These ways we must obey and follow always and correct ourselves when we do works that separates us from Jesus Christ.

Works we call sin, if you understand all good things belong to Our Heaven Father and the Kingdom of Heaven. Then we must also recognize all evil things belong to hell, and his serpent the devil, father of all lies and evildoing. Knowing that, unfaithfulness, hate, lies, selfishness, greed, disrespect, unforgiveness, vengeance, pride, adultery, murderous taught or actions, stealing, and all other wrongdoing are sins which then separate us from God's presence.

We must repent of our sins, confess in prayer to Our Heavenly

Father our sins, ask for His forgiveness, to be washed clean of our sins by Jesus Christ, Our Lord and Savior, by His grace and purpose, who redeemed us from sin on the cross, died, was buried, and resurrected from the dead on the third day as it is written in scripture. In:

- Matthew 22: 36-40

36 "Master, which is the great commandment in the law?"

37 "Jesus said unto him, Thou shalt love the Lord thy God with all thy heart, and with all thy soul, and with all thy mind."

38"This is the first and great commandment."

39"And the second is like unto it, Thou shalt love thy neighbor as thyself."

40"On these two commandments hang all the law and the prophet"

Chapter 7

Do You Truly Love GOD?

What Will Matter in the End!

What will matter in the end are not how many church services you attended, or the number of sermons you've preached. The only thing that will matter in the end is the extent to which you walked in love towards GOD, and men. The Ten Commandments can be summarized in love.

The first four commandments have to do with love for GOD, while the last six have to do with love for fellow humans.

So, today, you must ask yourself: Do you love GOD? Do you love Him? Do you honestly, truly love Him? Or do you just proclaim to love Him?

How do you know if you truly love Him? The Bible tells us in: -

John 14:15

"If ye love me, keep my commandments."

This is the judge of the world speaking. This is the head of the church speaking to us; all that matters is that you love Him. The evidence of the fact you love Him is you keep his commandments.

Loving Him is the first and greatest commandment. Loving Him is the biggest factor. It's not about how much you know the Bible, it's not about how much you attend church, and it's not about how much you know about prophecy. The biggest factor is, do you love GOD?

Loving GOD with all you heart, soul, and mind means GOD is at the core of your being. He is your heartbeat. All other relationships take a secondary role to your relations with Him. Loving GOD with all your heart, soul, and mind means you have allowed Him to flood the thoughts of your heart; you love Him with everything you have.

If you can get your thoughts off this world, and off yourself, and focus them on The LORD Jesus Christ, you will see what he has done for you. He first loved you, even when you were still a sinner; in your deliberate disobedience, He loved you.

Many of us confuse love for the things of GOD with a real passion for GOD. Love for the things of GOD does not automatically translate to love for GOD. It is possible to love church worship, or love church fellowship without really loving GOD. If all these things are taken away, GOD may not make sense to you anymore.

Loving GOD means loving Him for who He is, and all He has done for you.

Chapter 8
Giving Your Life to Christ

Many wonderful things happen to you when the Holy Spirit comes into your life; however, for a Christian, it does not end there. Once the Holy Spirit enters and dwells in you, He just doesn't stay unnoticed. He changes you from within. A change must take place. What this simply means is The Spirit of The Living GOD is now in you.

-Galatians 2:20 says:

"I am crucified with Christ: nevertheless, I live; yet not I, but Christ liveth in me: and the life which I now live in the flesh I live by the faith of the Son of God, who loved me, and gave himself for me."

This verse demonstrates the transformed life and the transitioning to Christ's life the moment you decide to "give your life to Christ."

If you have given your life to Christ, and there is no transformation in your life, whether subtle or evident, may I humbly suggest you question who is living in you!

Let us look at scripture and see what GOD says about a righteous and upright man: - Psalm 15:2 "He that walketh uprightly, and worketh righteousness, and speaketh the truth in his heart."

The truth about GOD is that He is a Holy GOD, whose eyes cannot behold inequity. The LORD desires us to work upright with Him. If we want to walk with Him, we have to align ourselves with Him, by being holy, He demands holiness from us; we see this in: – Matthew 5:48 "Be ye therefore perfect, even as your Father which is in heaven is perfect."

A person with the Holy Spirit begins the process of walking uprightly with GOD. Now, I am not suggesting the moment you are indwelt with the Holy Spirit you have arrived and everything becomes perfect. It's not a journey one sets out on to attain perfection; it's a continuous journey towards perfection and holiness.

Since we know in: – Romans 3:23-26

      23 "For all have sinned, and come short of the glory of God;"

      24 "Being justified freely by his grace through the redemption that is in Christ Jesus:"

      25 "Whom God hath set forth *to be* a propitiation through faith in his blood, to declare his righteousness for the remission of sins that are past, through the forbearance of God;"

      26 "To declare, *I say*, at this time his righteousness: that he might be just, and the justifier of him which believeth in Jesus."

One more verse from scripture to help grasp the concept can be found in:

Philippians 2:12

"Wherefore, my beloved, as ye have always obeyed, not as in my presence only, but now much more in my absence, work out your own salvation with fear and trembling."

The Word of GOD admonished believers to work out our own salvation with fear and trembling. It is a process that you begin to walk towards perfection. There is a clear progression.

What does it mean to be upright? Being upright is thinking right, walking right, talking right, doing the right things, and walking blamelessly before The LORD with a pure heart. That is one of the habits of a person with the Holy Spirit, their soul constantly yearns to do The Father's will, and do that which pleases Him.

There are no perfections in these areas, but progress and effort are needed to pull through.

- Hebrews 12:1

"Wherefore seeing we also are compassed about with so great a cloud of witnesses, let us lay aside every weight, and the sin which doth so easily beset *us*, and let us run with patience the race that is set before us."

The Christian life is a race. The writer of Hebrews said if we are going to run the Christian life with no distractions and not get off course, we must keep our eyes carefully focused on Jesus Christ. Since the Christian life is a race, let's examine the race course one must undertake, understanding very well the path is crucial to stay the course and not get lost along the way.

You see, my humble opinion on the concept of "running a Christian race" is as follows: All believers are running their own race at their own pace, depending on their devotion and passion to finish according to what they believe to be true.

Once again, in my humble opinion, I believe we are to run the race to reach the finish line, not to be the first one there, although we must not deviate from the course and lose track of our destination which is Jesus Christ our LORD and Savior. We must stay the course, remain focused on the path of the race, overcoming obstacles, or, as I like to call them "lessons" or "tests of faith."

One thing I have learned in my journey to Christ is once you truly give your life to Christ, acknowledge Him as your LORD and Savior, and aspire to be more as Christ taught us to be. The devil will hit you with everything he has to destabilize you and shake your faith with Jesus Christ.

The devil will attack your health, your mind, your family, your finances, your home, your surroundings; he will send temptations and opportunities meant to turn you away from Jesus Christ. The devil will create opportunities to present you with the occasion to lie, cheat, steal, kill, commit adultery, sexual immorality, bare false witness, act selfish; anything he has up his sleeve he will use to get you to sin.

He uses lies, deceit, and manipulation to get you to commit sin;

he can't force you, and can only try to convince you it's okay just this one time, it's not a big deal, no one will know. The devil tries to persuade you there are no consequences to sin, and in your moment of weakness, you give in to sin separating you from the presence of GOD, opening the door to the devil to swoop in and drag you further down into sin, hoping to crush your relationship with GOD the Father, The Son, and The Holy Spirit, known as The Holy Trinity.

If your faith in Jesus Christ is not laid upon a solid foundation, these things will shake your faith in GOD and crumble the Temple of GOD in you, leaving you vulnerable prey to the devil. It is written in scripture:

-1 Corinthians 10:12-13

> 12 "Wherefore let him that thinketh he standeth take heed lest he fall."
>
> 13 "There hath no temptation taken you but such as is common to man: but God *is* faithful, who will not suffer you to be tempted above that ye are able; but will with the temptation also make a way to escape, that ye may be able to bear *it*."

So you see, our Heavenly Father will allow obstacles to come our way for teaching to guide us, empower us, strengthen our faith, and sometimes, to even answer a prayer. For example: when you pray for patience, does He give you patience? Or the opportunity to be patient? When you pray for faithfulness, does he give you faithfulness? Or the opportunity to be faithful?

When you come to understand things don't happen to you, they happen for you, your whole perception changes on your struggles and misfortunes. You no longer see them as "curses" or "bad omens" meant to crush you, but to see your trials as "lessons," "corrections," and "opportunities" to increase your faith in The LORD.

Let's see what scripture teaches on this subject, if we head to:

- Romans 8:28

"And we know that all things work together for good to them that love God, to them who are the called according to *his* purpose."

We clearly see in this verse if you love The LORD, and if you are "called according to His purpose," all your trials and tribulations are working out according to the will of GOD, not to pull you down, but to raise you up; not to harm you, but to better you; not to weaken you, but to give you strength; not to hold you back, but increase your growth. It all comes back to perception. You can see problem in any solution, or you can see a solution to every problem. You can be grateful for what you have, or complain about what you don't have. You can be grateful the cup is half full, or see the cup as half empty; it all depends on your perception.

Now, with all this in mind, let's get back to the subject of running a Christian race. We know how it starts and we know how it finishes. For all of us, it begins when we receive Jesus Christ as our LORD and Savior and commit ourselves to the person of Jesus Christ. It's like getting married to Christ; that's the starting line.

Before you can run the race of life, you must start well. Of course, in between, the Bible says GOD has a race course for everyone that is planned out. Your course is different from mine, and mine is different from yours; different experiences, different places to go, and different things to do. But they have the same starting point, submission to Christ.

As we run the race of our Christian lives, we must run with our heads up and our eyes focused on Christ. If we choose to run the life of faith, we resist the distractions and look deeply into His eyes, keeping our eyes on Jesus, the source and perfector of our faith before the joy that was laid before Him, endured the cross, despised the shame, and is seated down the right hand of GOD's throne.

Jesus made Himself human and became a servant, the writer of Hebrews said in fact, if Jesus Christ can do it, you can to, because He didn't do this as GOD, He was doing this in His humanity. For the joy of saving us, He endured the cross, despising the shame.

Chapter 9
Knowing A Tree By Its Fruits

Now let us look at the fruit of the Spirit, we are taught once more in scripture in:

- Galatians 5:22

"But the fruit of the Spirit is love, joy, peace, longsuffering, gentleness, goodness, faith."

The fruit of the Spirit is the evidence someone has the Holy Spirit, but we are going to focus on faith. A habit of someone indwelled by the Holy Spirit is they live their life by faith.

2 Corinthians 1:24 says:

"Not for that we have dominion over your faith, but are helpers of your joy: for by faith ye stand." a person who is indwelt by the Holy Spirit stands by Faith. When the winds begin to blow and the storms of life begins to rage, we stand by Faith and not by sight.

But not only do we stand by faith, the Bible tells us, we must walk by faith.

-2 Corinthians 5:7

"(For we walk by faith, not by sight :), you cannot get away from this reality. Someone who is indwelt by the Holy Spirit is activated, to live a life of Faith.

2 Corinthians 4:13

"We having the same spirit of faith, according as it is written, I believed, and therefore have I spoken; we also believe, and therefore speak."

The word "spirit" here in this verse is written with a lowercase "s;" in other words, what Paul is saying is having the same viewpoint of faith, the same outlook of faith, Paul is saying, irrespective of all the things I have been through, GOD deposited within me a spirit of faith, and an outlook, and an attitude of faith. Hell through everything it had, but because of the spirit of Faith, I didn't give up, and I kept going on.

I personally believe although in this verse it is a lowercase "s," denoting and indicating the human spirit, we can translate this with a capital "S" which would make it the "Holy Spirit."

The Holy Spirit is acting and working on our spirits to give us an attitude of faith, and a Spirit of Faith so we can live a victorious life, and not a defeated one.

Faith is the foundation of all believers. Faith is the conduit by which we are saved, and faith is the avenue by which we actually receive the Holy Spirit. The Bible tells us, it is by faith that we please GOD according to: - Hebrews 11:6 "But without faith *it is* impossible to please *him*: for he that cometh to God must believe that he is, and *that* he is a rewarder of them that diligently seek him."

The habit of someone indwelt by the Holy Spirit is they live their life by faith. So, can we grow our faith so we can live a life of faith? Yes, we can, how? We are taught this in:

– Romans 10:17

"So then faith *cometh* by hearing, and hearing by the word of God."

You see, the word of GOD is made alive by the Holy Spirit, and when you begin to read the word of GOD, your faith begins to grow and the confidence the Holy Spirit gives you, is not that; that can only be used in church, but you will have faith you can apply in the real world. The Holy Spirit gives up the attitude of faith.

Chapter 10
Who Is the Holy Spirit?

Now the purpose of this chapter is to bring you into the knowledge of the person of the Holy Spirit, so you may be able to come into a complete relationship with Him, live with the reality of the indwelling GOD living within you, one with you, and you may hunger and thirst to yield all aspects of your life to Him, that you may be able to experience His love, His care, and His guidance.

The Holy Spirit is the third person of the Holy Trinity. The first is GOD the Father. The second is GOD the Son (Jesus Christ). The third is GOD the Holy Spirit. The Holy Spirit is probably the least of which people have an understanding. We know about our LORD and Savior Jesus Christ who was born of the Virgin Mary. We know about Almighty GOD the Father, the Creator of Heaven and Earth.

It is not hard to identify or have an understanding of GOD the Father, and Jesus Christ the Son of Almighty GOD, the Holy Spirit is the third member of the Holy Trinity. Correct doctrine of our LORD Jesus Christ is simple, and that is what we must follow. The doctrine is of love, and that he died for us on Calvary because of love. On the third day, He was resurrected, and He promised the Holy Spirit will give us power.

This is taught to us in: - Acts 1:8 "But ye shall receive power, after that the Holy Ghost is come upon you: and ye shall be witnesses unto me both in Jerusalem, and in all Judaea, and in Samaria, and unto the uttermost part of the earth."

I believe many Christians have gone to Calvary for pardon. Many of us have gone to Calvary for forgiveness of sin, but have failed to go to Pentecost for power. For us to receive power, we need to go to Pentecost. The first thing we must highlight is the reality the Holy Spirit is not an "it," but a "He." He is not a *thing*; He is not an *essence*; He is not a *power*, or even a *concept*. But he is a real person.

You see, if you think of the Holy Spirit as anything other than a person, it will be impossible for you to develop a relationship with the Holy Spirit. You cannot develop a relationship with a concept, or an essence, but you can develop a relationship with a person. Our LORD Jesus always referred to the Holy Spirit as a person: "He" or "Him."

He has been sent by The Father, at the request of Jesus, to come and live each day to help you and to be with you. He will be with you in your time of need. Now, if there were ever a group of men in a time of need, it was the disciples. These disciples were troubled and, in all honesty, they had every right to be troubled. Their world had just been shattered, because Jesus had told them: "one of you will betray me." That did not go down well with them.

Following that, He told them Peter was going to deny Him, and that hurt them because Peter was their leader. He was the strong one. Then, finally, He told them He was leaving. Jesus was leaving them, circumstances were against them, their enemies were against them, their friends were against them and on top of all that, Jesus was leaving,

Before He departed from the disciples, Jesus spoke about the "Comforter" who would be sent to us, meaning the Holy Spirit.

It is clearly expressed in; John 14: 16-18:
> 16 "And I will pray the Father, and he shall give you another Comforter, that he may abide with you forever;"
> 17 "*Even* the Spirit of truth; whom the world cannot receive, because it seeth him not, neither knoweth him: but ye know him; for he dwelleth with you, and shall be in you"
> 18 "I will not leave you comfortless: I will come to you."

What are the things the Holy Spirit will do for us?

One, He will teach us things. We believe we know all things, until they overwhelm us and we become powerless. When I was younger, I remember at some stage I genuinely believed I had life figured out. But the more I grew up, the more I found out there is more to this life than what I knew. We cannot know all things, because some things are spiritual. Our eyes cannot see beyond the physical, except when we are open to the spiritual.

This is what the Holy Spirit will do for us; He will teach us the things of the Spirit. Sometimes you read the Bible and it seems you cannot understand anything. The Holy Spirit will teach us the "Word of GOD;" the Holy Spirit will teach us the ways of GOD. The truth is, the things of GOD are spiritually discerned, and the Bible is a spiritual book. You cannot truly understand the Bible without the Holy Spirit.

You can be educated and not understand the Bible. You can be very intelligent and not understand the Bible. However, a person who may not be highly educated can be filled with the Holy Spirit and open the pages of the Bible and understand it. Understanding and reading the Bible has nothing to do with your intellect. You have a teacher who has opened your mind to spiritual things, and one of those spiritual things is the "Word of GOD;" the Bible.

The Holy Spirit will not just teach us things, but also remind us of the things of GOD we had never learned.

Secondly, He is the comforter, as taught in: John 14:16: "And I will pray the Father, and he shall give you another Comforter, that he may abide with you forever." This word, the comforter, has been gravely misunderstood. When we have the Holy Spirit as our comforter, we think of him as our "cuddle buddy;" we think of Him as a soft safety net to protect us from the challenges of life. This is incorrect. In Latin, the word "*com*" means "with," and "*fort*" means "strength."

Did you hear the Holy Spirit is there to come with strength? Are you tired and weary? You need more of the Holy Spirit. Are you broken and alone? You need more of the Holy Spirit.

So, I encourage you today, by writing this chapter, to let you know we need the Holy Spirit of GOD. We all know the Holy Spirit is the comforter; however, the original Greek word that was used is the "Parakletos;" "*Para*" meaning "alongside," and "*kletos*" meaning "to call." In other words, the Holy Spirit is one called alongside to help.

However, we have a very limited view of the Holy Spirit. We see the Holy Spirit as the comforter, who comes alongside when were really heartbroken, and wraps us up in something soft, nice, warm, and gives us a big hug. This is not true. The word "comforter" has changed its meaning overtime. Today, if you say "I will comfort you," invariably what you mean is "I will get you out of trouble;" "I will get you away from situations;" "I will get you away from anything causing you to bother."

But, in fact, the word "comforter" originally meant exactly the opposite. It meant *to put someone right in the middle of the battle and give them the strength they needed to face it.* It comes from the Latin word "*Fortis*" where we get the word "fortified," "fortification;" it means *to be put right in the middle of the battle and equipped, and fashioned, and formed with the strength you need to overcome and to win.*

I encourage you to ask The LORD for the Holy Spirit; He is the Spirit of Power. Whatever you are facing at this time, the Holy Spirit will give you the strength not to run away from it, but to face up to it. The Holy Spirit will give you the power. Jesus didn't send the Spirit of Truth so we could be defeated; defeated with our challenges, defeated with emotional challenges, defeated with spiritual challenges. The Spirit of Truth came to give you the power to face anything in your life today.

Presently, we must seek for another level connection with the Holy Spirit; this will send a jolt of power into the call of our being. Power comes when the Spirit of man or woman are connected with the Spirit of GOD. You don't have to face the battles of life alone; GOD is giving you the provision of the Holy Spirit.

In other words, what the Holy Spirit does is, rather than coming into your life to hide you from facing challenges, the Holy Spirit allows you to join in fellowship with Him, and He strengthens you during that time. Once you are strong enough again, He sends you out again with strength to face the challenges of life.

The Holy Spirit isn't there to be a babysitter, where the baby cries, He picks you up, and says, "There, there, honey, let me take all your troubles away." But rather, "You are going through some trouble; come, here is some strength; now back to the battle."

He also shows us secrets; we see that in: -

1 Corinthians 2:10
"But God hath revealed *them* unto us by his Spirit: for the Spirit searcheth all things, yea, the deep things of God."

The things we cannot see with our eyes, the Holy Spirit reveals them to us in the Spirit. There is more to this life than physical things; things that happen in the physical are the results of things done in the spiritual. For us to be able to take on the forces around us, we must be able to see them in the spirit, and take control of the spiritual. This is what the Holy Spirit will do for us. We will see the things that we need to see.

GOD wants us to know there are secrets, but we can't get them without His Spirit. The Holy Spirit searches GOD and tells us every-thing. This makes us superior in life, and we've become powerful by the power of GOD.

The Holy Spirit is a being; He is GOD in man. We need the Holy Spirit in us as Christians so we can carry the power of GOD in us.

Chapter 11
What It Means to "Walk in the Spirit"

Step one, let's begin this chapter with scripture to lay a foundation to help you understand a few of many verses in the Bible which relate to the teachings of "being in the Spirit" or "walking in the Spirit."

I have listened to many different opinions and theories on this subject; some of them are more accurate than others. But, after all, who am I to judge? This is simply my humble opinion. I will do my best to share what I found in scripture about "being and walking in the Spirit." So here we go. If we look at scripture in:

- Romans 8:5

"For they that are after the flesh do mind the things of the flesh; but they that are after the Spirit the things of the Spirit."

Life in the Spirit is a journey, and while many great passages through-out scriptures discusses the role and person of the Holy Spirit, this verse I find to be the most insightful.

Sometimes, the Holy Spirit leads us directly; the Holy Spirit can choose to act in any way and according to any timetable that he wishes. We do not dictate to Him how or when He will move. Since the Bible gives many examples of Him acting more specifically, we should antic-ipate He will sometimes choose to lead us directly if we are open and available to His guidance.

But how can you live a life directed by the Holy Spirit and fuel a passion for the things of the Spirit? We find steps in the previous verse, set your mind on the things of the Spirit. The question is, how does one overcome the pull of the flesh? Sounds like an old riddle.

How can someone extract all the air out of a drinking glass? The most direct way to get all the air out of a glass is by filling it with something else. You cannot extract thoughts that displease GOD from your mind, like the solution to the riddle; you need to be filled with thoughts, indeed, with an entire mindset all oriented towards the things of the Spirit.

This is what I believe to be the meaning of "walking in the Spirit." First, you must be filled with the Holy Spirit, I believe this happens when you are "born again;" the moment you truly give your life to Christ. Once you are washed of your inequities, by the purpose and blood of Jesus Christ our LORD and Savior, you become a new creation, worthy to receive the presence of the Holy Spirit.

From that day forward, you no longer want to please the world or the pleasures of the flesh, but instead thirst for the Spirit of the Father, the Son, and the Holy Spirit. This is the day you truly humble yourself before Almighty GOD and decide to learn and be made aware of the laws, teachings, and commandments, first. Then apply what you are taught in scripture and teachings to all things you do which will ultimately change the way you view the world which, in my humble opinion, means you are "walking in accordance to the Spirit of GOD" which I believe to be very similar, if not the same as "walking in the Spirit." When His ways and commandments are the essence in which you conduct yourself and interact with the world.

That very moment, you are "born again;" you are gifted with the presence of the Holy Spirit, sent to minister to you, guide you, and give you strength and courage, and power to carry on, no matter what the obstacle(s) present, or the ones who are to come, if you trust in the Holy Spirit, trust also He will help you, and guide you through your troubled times.

If we look at:

– Romans 12:2

"And be not conformed to this world: but be ye transformed by the renewing of your mind, that ye may prove what *is* that good, and acceptable, and perfect, will of God."

You need to fill your mind with GOD's thoughts, fill your mind with things of the Spirit. The Bible is a spiritual book, and the words in this book are spiritual food we can fill our minds with and live by its teachings.

In: - Matthew 4:4, it is written:

"But he answered and said, It is written, Man shall not live by bread alone, but by every word that proceedeth out of the mouth of God.", knowing that the Bible is a spiritual book, and without the Holy Spirit, you will never be able to understand the Bible. The Bible has nothing to do with your intellect; it has to do with your spirit, the inner man.

Therefore, without the Holy Spirit, you can read the Bible and it won't have the same effect as someone with the Holy Spirit who reads the Bible.

We can see an example of this in: - 2 Timothy 3:16-17

16 "All scripture *is* given by inspiration of God, and *is* profitable for doctrine, for reproof, for correction, for instruction in righteousness:"

17 "That the man of God may be perfect, thoroughly furnished unto all good works."

With this understanding, we must renew our minds and focus to allow ourselves to be guided by the Holy Spirit; we need to know the word of GOD. For you to become a complete man or woman of GOD, you need to know the word of GOD. There is no substitute for the word of GOD. The Bible is our reference point; it's the anchor to our soul.

The more and more you read the word of GOD, and receive it, the process of renewal of your mind begins. When you read the word of GOD, you begin to realize GOD doesn't make any mistakes. You begin to think like GOD, to love what GOD loves.

In order to know how GOD wants you to live, you must know

His word, and if you want to know what GOD thinks of you, we must study His word. The word of GOD has power to renew your mind and soul, but it needs to get inside you. Once it gets inside of you, there's a transformation that takes place.

Is sin a struggle in your daily life? Do you find it hard to resist sin? The Bible has the answer to your struggles, big or small. Are you brokenhearted and lonely? In the Bible, you will find The LORD who *loves* you and *cares* for you. Someone who would give their life for you, in fact, He already gave His life for you, our LORD and Savior Jesus Christ.

We have proof of this in:

- John 3:16

"For God so loved the world that he gave his only begotten Son, that whosoever believeth in him should not perish, but have everlasting life."

That is who you will find in the Bible. That is the kind of love you can have. We don't deserve it, but it's been given to us.

Scripture has the power to renew your mind. If your thoughts about yourself are how you are not good enough, or not smart enough, or not beautiful enough, I encourage you to discover what the word of GOD says about you and renew your mind.

It is written in: – Genesis 1:27

"So God created man in his *own* image, in the image of God created he him; male and female created he them."

You were not created by accident; you didn't randomly come into being. GOD created you; you're not a random misfit that just happened to be born. GOD specifically created you.

Step two; put to death the deeds of the body by the Spirit. In other words, say "no" to your desires. This was taught to us in the word of GOD. Once again, scripture is provided to explain what this means.

If we look at: - Romans 8:12-15, it says:

12 "Therefore, brethren, we are debtors, not to the flesh, to live

after the flesh."

13 "For if ye live after the flesh, ye shall die: but if ye through the Spirit do mortify the deeds of the body, ye shall live."

14 "For as many as are led by the Spirit of God, they are the sons of God."

15 "For ye have not received the spirit of bondage again to fear; but ye have received the Spirit of adoption, whereby we cry, Abba, Father."

He or she who has been rejuvenated by the Spirit is not stuck in sin. By the Spirit, the desires of the flesh can be resisted. It is possible, by the help of GOD's Spirit, to say "no" to your desires and temptations. It's pretty similar to saying no to sin, but just saying "no" by itself will never be successful. Just saying "no" will never allow you to overcome sin consistently.

Then what must you do? You might ask, where's the special ingredient to overcome desires of the flesh consistently? You must say "no" by the Spirit.

Step three, you are now walking in the Spirit, keeping in mind the verse previously mentioned: -Roman 8:14, which said, "For as many as are led by the Spirit of God, they are the sons of God."

The Holy Spirit leads us broadly, always, and more specifically, sometimes. He always guides us through the written word of GOD, which was revealed to the prophets by the Holy Spirit.

Scripture teaches us this in: - 2 Peter 1:20-21, which is:

20 "Knowing this first, that no prophecy of the scripture is of any private interpretation."

21 "For the prophecy came not in old time by the will of man: but holy men of God spake *as they were* moved by the Holy Ghost"

We are to prayerfully, carefully, and humbly apply deep Biblical wisdom to the situations we face in our lives.

Chapter 12
Praying in the Spirit

Sadly, this is a subject many Christians seem to overlook or forget. I will do my best to explain what this actually means. Focusing on scripture, always, if we navigate to: - Romans 8:26-28

26 "Likewise the Spirit also helpeth our infirmities: for we know not what we should pray for as we ought: but the Spirit itself maketh intercession for us with groanings which cannot be uttered."

27 "And he that searcheth the hearts knoweth what *is* the mind of the Spirit, because he maketh intercession for the saints according to *the will of* God."

28 "And we know that all things work together for good to them that love God, to them who are the called according to *his* purpose."

We know we are weak when we come to prayer. We often do not know what to pray for, in any given situation. The concern is not about the manner of prayer, the "how," but rather the content of our prayers. What do we actually pray about?

We learn that the Spirit joins to help us when we are struggling to know how to pray by interceding for us with wordless groaning. It is not as some propose we should just pray whatever we want since we don't have any idea on how to pray, and the Spirit fixes them on our behalf to The Father.

Rather, the verb often translated as "help" has a preposition attached to the front of it, which suggests it really means "joins to help." The Spirit is searching our hearts and knows we have a mindset focused

65

on Him. Even if we do not know exactly what we are supposed to pray, the result is our prayers are prayed, according to the will of GOD.

Because the Holy Spirit is moving us thus to pray, and He is presenting us the prayer He is guiding us to pray to The Father.

Conclusion

Prayer is certainly one of the greatest privileges we have as believers. Whatever we take full advantage of this privilege is another issue. We have, as believers, a fellowship with The Father. It is a medium of communication to Him.

When teaching the disciples to pray, Jesus taught them in this order. I will use verses from Matthew 6:9-13:

> 9 "After this manner therefore pray ye: Our Father which art in heaven, Hallowed be thy name"
> 10 "Thy kingdom come, thy will be done in earth, as *it is* in heaven."
> 11 "Give us this day our daily bread"
> 12 "And forgive us our debts, as we forgive our debtors."
> 13 "And lead us not into temptation, but deliver us from evil: For thine is the" kingdom, and the power, and the glory, forever. Amen."

Prayer subjects up to The Fatherhood of GOD, prayer energizes us to do the will of The Father. As a matter of fact, prayer is a necessity in our Christian walk with GOD. Pray in the good times, pray in the bad times, pray in your troubled times, and pray in you blessed times. Pray every chance you get.

Pray as a child to a loving Father, pray as a victor and not as a victim, pray with love and not with hate, pray with faith and hope not doubt and fear, pray humbly not with arrogance, pray for the ones you love, but pray also for your enemies, pray when you wake in the morning, and pray as you head to sleep at night. Prayer is a very powerful tool for any believer and non-believer. Prayer opens the hearts of anyone willing to experience the love and greatness of GOD the Father, the

Son Jesus Christ, and the Holy Spirit, known as the Holy Trinity, that is why prayer must be part of our daily lives, always, without ceasing.

Apostle Paul acknowledged this in: 1 Thessalonians 5:17-18
>   17 "Pray without ceasing."
>   18 "In everything give thanks: for this is the will of God in Christ Jesus concerning you."

What then does it mean to pray in the Spirit, praying in the Spirit is relying on The Spirit of GOD to help us in the place of prayer. Like a puzzle Paul rightly said in; – Romans 8:26 "Likewise the Spirit also helpeth our infirmities: for we know not what we should pray for as we ought: but the Spirit itself maketh intercession for us with groanings which cannot be uttered."

Praying in the Spirit is giving up one self to governorship of the Holy Spirit, because we do not know the will of The Father. Therefore, we need an intercessor to mediate on our behalf. We must understand that all prayer is accepted based on intercession. Praying in the Spirit is received through faith in Jesus Christ.

We are taught this also in: – Ephesians 6:18 which say: "Praying always with all prayer and supplication in the Spirit, and watching thereunto with all perseverance and supplication for all saints."

With this in mind, be alert, and always keep on praying for all The LORD's people.

Here are two more examples in scripture which teach us on this subject, so you can fully understand what I am trying to convey on this matter.

Jude 1:20 "But ye, beloved, building up yourselves on your most holy faith, praying in the Holy Ghost."

1 Corinthians 14:15 "What is it then? I will pray with the spirit, and I will pray with the understanding also: I will sing with the spirit, and I

will sing with the understanding also."
Brother or sister soul, most of us don't understand these verses, at least many of us don't. If we did, we would pray more, we would make prayer the principal thing in our life. Each of the verses lays emphasis on the importance of "praying in the Spirit." Praying in the Spirit is a prayer of the believer backed up by the power of The Holy Spirit to communicate with our Heavenly Father.

Every believer is expected to pray in the Spirit as an act of intimacy with The Father. Praying in the Spirit keeps you in the constant state of your position in Christ Jesus, without condemnation, and equally emboldens you as an heir of GOD, and joint heir with Christ.

Psalm 38:9 "Lord, all my desire *is* before thee; and my groaning is not hid from thee."

He hears your groaning; He hears the Holy Spirit which intercedes for you. This word "intercede" means to "plead, speak on behalf of another, mediate, arbitrate, and intervene." The Holy Spirit is doing all this for you.

I really hope this chapter helped you understand who The Holy Spirit truly is, and the meaning of walking and praying in the Spirit. Always remember, prayer must be done in private. I have seen many different opinions and discussions on this topic, many points of views, and many interpretations.

I will offer you my humble opinion on this topic and you can decide if it makes sense to you or not. I'm not saying my point of view is better than any other, but this is what I believe to be true to me, so once again, this is my humble opinion on praying privately, or publicly.

It is never bad or wrong to acknowledge The LORD in public with your peers, worship The LORD in public, celebrate The LORD in public, glorify The LORD in public, sing to The LORD in public, speak and teach of The LORD in public. These are all great things in the eyes of our Heavenly Father.

But when it comes to prayer, I humbly believe it must be done in private, and here is why I believe this. Scripture has an answer for every question one might have and this topic is no different. Although we can argue on its definition, some topics are quite clear.

Relying on scripture, the word of GOD, meant to teach us and guide us, it is written in:

- Matthew 6:5-6:

5 "And when thou prayest, thou shalt not be as the hypocrites are: for they love to pray standing in the synagogues and in the corners of the streets, that they may be seen of men. Verily I say unto you, they have their reward."

6 "But thou, when thou prayest, enter into thy closet, and when thou hast shut thy door, pray to thy Father which is in secret; and thy Father which seeth in secret shall reward thee openly."

Looking at these two verses, we can clearly determine praying must be confined to be done in private, away from distractions, away from anything that would interrupt you from having "quality time" by speaking to our Heavenly Father in prayer, by praying in the Spirit, meaning "speaking with our inner voice."

Chapter 13
Praying Against the Devil and His Schemes

In this chapter, we will be looking through Scripture to see how the devil is described in the Bible. My intention is to make you aware of who the devil really is so you can be equipped to resist his schemes and temptations. This chapter in no way glorifies the devil, but to expose him and to empower you, to give you knowledge on who is trying to pull you away from our LORD and Savior Jesus Christ and salvation.

Knowing your enemy is the first step to overcome him. So, based on scripture and what I have learned by personal experience, listening and researching different point of views on this matter, I will attempt to demonstrate what I humbly believe to be true, depending on my understanding and knowledge acquired during my process of learning the word of GOD and wanting to be more like Christ.

As a believer and humble Christian who gave my life to Jesus Christ, I wanted to know the teachings and guidance that comes from scripture, but I also understood the fact the devil is real, and we should be aware of who he is and how to protect ourselves with prayer and with the power of the name of Jesus Christ our LORD and Savior.

Now let me tell you about the devil first so you've got a clear picture in your mind of what we're praying against. First, the Bible does not paint him as a horned creature with a forked tail; that's the type of depiction that makes people laugh, and take him less seriously. Scripture describes him as a fallen angel, a real person, walking amongst us, searching for prey to devour.

We see an example of this in: - 1 Peter 5:8

"Be sober-minded; be watchful. Your adversary the devil prowls around like a roaring lion, seeking someone to devour."

Also in: – Job 1:7

"And the LORD said unto Satan, Whence comest thou? Then Satan answered the LORD, and said, from going to and fro in the earth, and from walking up and down in it."

Scripture never calls the devil it, always he. Scripture also teaches us he has a heart, a mind, and a will. If these three elements don't consist a personality, I don't know what does. Scripture talks about the devil's feelings, talks about his thoughts, and about his motives. My understanding on such things clearly portrays a real person.

The devil is not just a kind of vague word to sum up all the forces of evil in the world. No, he is a real person in his own right, and if there were no human beings at all, the devil would still exist.

Jesus Himself took the devil seriously. He never made a joke about him. He never laughed at him, He never caricaturized him. Here are some of the titles Jesus gave the devil in Scripture: He said he was the prince of this world. We are taught this in Scripture.

An example of this: - Ephesians 2:2-4

2 "in which you once walked, following the course of this world, following the prince of the power of the air, the spirit that is now at work in the sons of disobedience"

3 "among whom we all once lived in the passions of our flesh, carrying out the desires of the body and the mind, and were by nature children of wrath, like the rest of mankind.

4 "But[c] God, being rich in mercy, because of the great love with which he loved us,"

When the devil offered Jesus all the kingdoms of the world, Jesus did not say "they are not yours to give" because He knew perfectly well, they were the devil's to give. We see this in; - Matthew 4:8-10

8 "Again, the devil taketh him up into an exceeding high mountain, and sheweth him all the kingdoms of the world, and the glory of them;"

9 "And saith unto him, all these things will I give thee, if thou wilt fall down and worship me."

10 "Then saith Jesus unto him, get thee hence, Satan: for it is written, Thou shalt worship the Lord thy God, and him only shalt thou serve."

It's a horrible thought if you truly realize the world in which we live is ruled over by the devil; he is the prince of this world, but let me take this further. Do you know another title Scripture gave the devil? Not only described him as "ruler" or "prince of this world," he is "god of this world." We see this taught in: - 2 Corinthians 4:4 "In whom the god of this world hath blinded the minds of them which believe not, lest the light of the glorious gospel of Christ, who is the image of God, should shine unto them."

We must recognize when the word "god" is used to describe the devil, it is in a lowercase "g." There is only one GOD, our Father in Heaven, He is Alpha and Omega, the Beginning and the End, the First and the Last, Creator and Master of all things. But let me explain, in my humble opinion, on why I believe Scripture defines the devil "god of this world."

My understanding is, not only that the devil controls this world and is able to manipulate science, education, and politics for his own ends. More than that, the devil is actually the god most people on earth worship, whether they know it or not.

Behind so much religion, behind so many activities, the devil is the one who's being worshipped; he's the one.

Even by some who go to church and chapel on Sunday. In reality he's their god. For they worship the things that he offers them, they want the things of the world, that he belongs to, and rule over, rather than setting their mind on the things that are above where Jesus is.

If you are seeking things of the flesh, things of this world, then the devil is your god. Let's bring back a previously mentioned verse that teaches us on this said subject.

1 John 2:15-16

15 "Love not the world, neither the things *that are* in the world. If any man love the world, the love of the Father is not in him."

16 "For all that *is* in the world, the lust of the flesh, and the lust of the eyes, and the pride of life, is not of the Father, but is of the world."

If you are prioritizing things of this world, knowingly or unknowingly, you are worshiping the devil, making him your god; he will give it to you, there's always a price to pay. When the bill comes in, you might not be quite so happy, but he'll give it to you. He can give you money, he can give you fame, he can give you anything you want on earth, because it's his to give.

Now, let's get this clear: that doesn't mean GOD is helpless in this world. It does mean, and we're got to think this through, GOD is allowing the devil to be prince of this world. GOD the Father allowed it. Some might say, "What does GOD think He's doing allowing the devil to be prince of the world?" Well, my response to that would be: "What's he doing allowing you to be like you are?" Why should you blame The LORD for allowing the devil to rebel, when The LORD allowed you to be free to choose your path, therefore choosing your destination?

The answer is quite simple: GOD Almighty is our Father, and He will not force any of His creations to go His way, and GOD gives you freedom the freedom to choose. We can't grumble about The LORD giving the angels freedom, though they have superior intelligence and strength, due to the fact The LORD granted all of us the same freedom to choose: either you follow Jesus Christ or you willingly or unwillingly follow the devil and things of the flesh.

Do you know there are two books in the Bible the devil truly hates more than any other out of all sixty-six?

There are two that say more about him than any others, and it's these the devil has attacked more than any others. They are the one of the beginning and the one at the end, Genesis and Revelation, and you know why the devil hates them?

Genesis teaches us of his devices and schemes, and Revelation teaches us about his destination and doom. He hates those two books, and there have been more scholarly attacks on the book of Genesis than any other book, and more attempt to turn it into myth and legend, and away from fact, than any other book in the Bible.

Why? Because the devil doesn't want you to believe Genesis 3 ever happened. He doesn't want you to know how he got hold of Eve, and he doesn't want you to believe what he did to that first married couple. Genesis teaches us about Creation and the "purpose of creation," it also teaches us about disobedience to GOD and the fall (separation) of Adam and Eve from GOD. He attacks the book of Genesis with all he has to make you be blind to what it teaches.

The other book he hates more than any other is the book of Revelation. As you read through Scripture in the book of Revelation, you come to a point where it teaches the devil himself will be cast in the lake of fire, also known as "bottomless pit" or "pit of hell."

Are you aware Jesus told us to pray daily for protection against the devil and his schemes? The original prayer Jesus taught His disciples when they said, "LORD teach us to pray" as seen in:

- Luke 11:1

"And it came to pass, that, as he was praying in a certain place, when he ceased, one of his disciples said unto him, Lord, teach us to pray, as John also taught his disciples."

Then Jesus told the disciples to acknowledge GOD the Father and things He wants, His name, His will, and His kingdom, in:

- Luke 11:2

"And he said unto them, when ye pray, say, Our Father which art in heaven, Hallowed be thy name. Thy kingdom come. Thy will be done, as in heaven, so in earth."

Followed by things we need: we need food, we need forgiveness, we need fortitude and strength to resist temptation, then Jesus told them to pray for deliverance from evil, meaning the evil one, in:

- Luke 11:3-4

> 3 "Give us day by day our daily bread."
>
> 4 "And forgive us our sins; for we also forgive every one that is indebted to us. And lead us not into temptation; but deliver us from evil."

We've turned evil into a thing in our perception. It is not a thing, and he is a person. There is no evil anywhere in all creation apart from persons or beings that do evil; evil is an intensely personal thing. There is no love in creation apart from persons and beings who love. So evil is personal.

Jesus said to pray daily "deliver me from the evil one."

Start your prayer by thinking of your Father in Heaven, and end your prayer by thinking of the devil on earth, and go out to face him.

The devil has many names as seen in: – Revelation 12:9 "And the great dragon was cast out, that old serpent, called the Devil, and Satan, which deceiveth the whole world: he was cast out into the earth, and his angels were cast out with him."

The devil is also a murderer and liar, and not just any liar, the father of all lies.

We see this in: - John 8:44 "Ye are of *your* father the devil, and the lusts of your father ye will do. He was a murderer from the beginning, and abode not in the truth, because there is no truth in him. When he speaketh a lie, he speaketh of his own: for he is a liar, and the father of it."

If you lie or kill or sin, you are making the devil your father, therefore your god.

If our Heavenly Father allowed His Beloved Son Jesus Christ, our LORD and Savior, to be tempted by the devil, don't you think GOD the Father will also allow each one of us to go through the same "test of Faith"? We must remember the teaching in:

- John 17:15

"I pray not that thou shouldest take them out of the world, but that thou shouldest keep them from the evil."

We will be tempted, we will be tested, but if you stand strong in faith, you will overcome. The purpose of the devil is to steal, kill, and destroy. We see this taught in:

- John 10:10

"The thief cometh not, but for to steal, and to kill, and to destroy: I am come that they might have life, and that they might have *it* more abundantly."

Chapter 14

Put on the "Full Armor of GOD"

As a believer of Jesus Christ, you must come to the understanding we are in a spiritual battle, clearly taught in:

- Ephesians 6:10-17 -The Full Armor of God-

> 10 "Finally, my brethren, be strong in the Lord, and in the power of his might."
>
> 11 "Put on the whole armour of God that ye may be able to stand against the wiles of the devil."
>
> 12 "For we wrestle not against flesh and blood, but against principalities, against powers, against the rulers of the darkness of this world, against spiritual wickedness in high *places*."
>
> 13 "Wherefore take unto you the whole armour of God that ye may be able to withstand in the evil day, and having done all, to stand."
>
> 14 "Stand therefore, having your loins girt about with truth, and having on the breastplate of righteousness;"
>
> 15 "And your feet shod with the preparation of the gospel of peace;"
>
> 16 "Above all, taking the shield of faith, wherewith ye shall be able to quench all the fiery darts of the wicked."
>
> 17 "And take the helmet of salvation, and the sword of the Spirit, which is the word of God:"

The enemy the devil and his minions are waging war, seeking the destruction of Almighty GOD the Father's creation, which means all of us. The devil will use every tool possible to persuade you to sin; he will lie to you in whispers, he will manipulate you into sin if you let him, he will deceive you if you let him, he will try to interfere with your pursuit for Jesus Christ, and he will try to separate you from the Grace and Mercy of Almighty GOD.

We are to be courageous and bold when it comes to facing the forces of darkness in this world. Fear and despair are not an option in this manner; defeat is not an option for anyone seeking the mighty gift of salvation and eternal life in the purpose of Jesus Christ our Lord and Savior. Alone you will fail, but with the protection and power in the name of Jesus Christ, the enemy the devil will flee from you.

Taught in: - James 4:7

"Submit yourselves therefore to God. Resist the devil, and he will flee from you."

No weapon formed against you will prosper, clearly taught in:

- Isaiah 54:17

"No weapon that is formed against thee shall prosper; and every tongue *that* shall rise against thee in judgment thou shalt condemn. This *is* the heritage of the servants of the LORD, and their righteousness *is* of me, saith the LORD."

If you truly believe in The LORD, act accordingly, if you believe in the power and protection of Almighty GOD, act accordingly. If you seek to have a relationship with Jesus, act accordingly. If you seek the grace and mercy of The LORD, act accordingly. If you seek salvation and eternal life, act accordingly. If you claim to love Almighty GOD, act accordingly. If you claim to fear The LORD, act accordingly.

We are taught many times in Scripture not to fear anything, here are two examples chosen from many, the first would be:

- Psalm 23:4

"Yea, though I walk through the valley of the shadow of death, I will fear no evil: for thou *art* with me; thy rod and thy staff they comfort me."

The second example I selected can be found in: -

Psalm 91:1-16 - My Refuge and My Fortress

1 "He that dwelleth in the secret place of the most High shall abide under the shadow of the Almighty."

2 "I will say of the LORD, *He is* my refuge and my fortress: my God; in him will I trust."

3 "Surely he shall deliver thee from the snare of the fowler, *and* from the noisome pestilence."

4 "He shall cover thee with his feathers, and under his wings shalt thou trust: his truth *shall be thy* shield and buckler."

5 "Thou shalt not be afraid for the terror by night; *nor* for the arrow *that* flieth by day;"

6 "*Nor* for the pestilence *that* walketh in darkness; *nor* for the destruction *that* wasteth at noonday."

7 "A thousand shall fall at thy side, and ten thousand at thy right hand; *but* it shall not come nigh thee."

8 "Only with thine eyes shalt thou behold and see the reward of the wicked."

9 "Because thou hast made the LORD, *which is* my refuge, *even* the most High, thy habitation;"

10 "There shall no evil befall thee, neither shall any plague come nigh thy dwelling."

11 "For he shall give his angels charge over thee, to keep thee in all thy ways."

12 "They shall bear thee up in *their* hands, lest thou dash thy foot against a stone."

13 "Thou shalt tread upon the lion and adder: the young lion

and the dragon shalt thou trample under feet. "

14 "Because he hath set his love upon me, therefore will I deliver him: I will set him on high, because he hath known my name."

15 "He shall call upon me, and I will answer him: I *will be* with him in trouble; I will deliver him, and honour him."

16 "With long life will I satisfy him, and shew him my salvation."

Fear of Almighty GOD is the only fear allowed for a true believer of Jesus Christ, taught in; - Psalms 111:10 "The fear of the LORD *is* the beginning of wisdom: a good understanding have all they that do *his commandments*: his praise endureth forever."

Once you acquire wisdom, keep it close to you and she will prosper you, clearly taught in:

- Proverbs 3:13-23 - Blessed is He who Finds Wisdom

13 "Happy *is* the man *that* findeth wisdom, and the man *that* getteth understanding."

14 "For the merchandise of it *is* better than the merchandise of silver, and the gain thereof than fine gold."

15 "She *is* more precious than rubies: and all the things thou canst desire are not to be compared unto her."

16 "Length of days *is* in her right hand; *and* in her left hand riches and honour."

17 "Her ways *are* ways of pleasantness, and all her paths *are* peace."

18 "She *is* a tree of life to them that lay hold upon her: and happy *is every one* that retaineth her."

19 "The LORD by wisdom hath founded the earth; by understanding hath he established the heavens."

20 "By his knowledge the depths are broken up, and the clouds drop down the dew."

21 "My son, let not them depart from thine eyes: keep sound wisdom and discretion:"

22 "So shall they be life unto thy soul, and grace to thy neck."

23 "Then shalt thou walk in thy way safely, and thy foot shall not stumble."

Since we are in a spiritual battle for our souls, we must be equipped for such a battle to overcome the enemy and his schemes.

Scripture teaches us about putting on the full armor of GOD. Without this armor, the devil will overcome you and drag you with him to his final destination, of which he is very well aware. He knows the bottomless pit awaits him. His goal is to drag you down with him, clearly taught in:

Revelation 20:7-10 - Satan Cast into the Lake of Fire

7 "And when the thousand years are expired, Satan shall be loosed out of his prison,"

8 "And shall go out to deceive the nations which are in the four quarters of the earth, Gog and Magog, to gather them together to battle: the number of whom *is* as the sand of the sea."

9 "And they went up on the breadth of the earth, and compassed the camp of the saints about, and the beloved city: and fire came down from God out of heaven, and devoured them."

10 "And the devil that deceived them was cast into the lake of fire and brimstone, where the beast and the false prophet *are*, and shall be tormented day and night for ever and ever."

I will humbly do my best, based on my knowledge and understanding, to express what I discovered in Scripture on what it means to "put on the full armor of GOD." Always relying on the written word of GOD taught to whoever seeks wisdom in Scripture.

First, we must understand in a spiritual battle you need a spiritual armor. Not an actual physical armor; the armor is composed of different elements for different purposes to use in this battle we face. Equipped with this armor, the enemy is powerless and already defeated in the name, purpose, and power of Jesus Christ our LORD and Savior, which has already defeated the enemy for all of us when He took upon Himself the sins of the whole world, as taught in:

- Revelation 1:5

"And from Jesus Christ, *who is* the faithful witness, *and* the first begotten of the dead, and the prince of the kings of the earth. Unto him that loved us, and washed us from our sins in his own blood"

Now, let's examine in detail the elements required to put on the full armor of GOD.

First component: Helmet of Salvation: "Your salvation should always be at the forefront of your mind; it will keep your priorities in order."

Second component: Breastplate or Righteousness: "You have an upright heart, morally erect; having the rightness of principles and conduct, being honest and just, you are seeking to do the true will of the Father."

Third component; Belt (girdle) of Truth "Having this belt means you have the moral courage to stand up for what is right and stand against what is wrong. No matter what, stand your ground."

Fourth component: Sword of the Spirit: "Your only weapon is the Word of GOD, the Scriptures of the Bible, this is how you fight, all the other pieces are armor, but the Scriptures are your weapon, so you must know them."

Fifth component: Shield of Faith: "Is lifted up to protect you, and to extinguish all the flaming arrows of the evil one, you must have your shield of Faith because this is what gets tested the most."

Sixth component: the Boots of the Gospel: "The shoes prepare you to face the enemy with firm-footed stability and a readiness that is only produced by the Gospel."

You see, the devil will try to make you feel fear, dirty, shameful, worthless, without reason or purpose, alone, sad, unhappy, hopeless, defenseless, and so on. Society has led us to believe acquiring things of this world in mass will fill the emptiness we feel inside, and for some reason, the more we acquire, the emptier we feel.

In my humble opinion, and based upon what I learned in Scripture, that which slowly fills the emptiness cannot be bought, borrowed, lent. You cannot see it, or touch it, its value holds no price tag here on earth, and its true value has no equal.

I'm speaking of faith, love, kindness, compassion, respect, understanding, patience, and so on, all positive things. Morals and principles of a true believer and follower of our LORD and Savior Jesus Christ, who taught us, and displayed it by being the perfect example on how to conduct ourselves in order to please our Heavenly Father.

You see, I follow the Ten Commandments and the teachings of Jesus Christ my LORD and Savior; He is the way, the truth, and the life, clearly taught in:

- John 14:6

"Jesus saith unto him, I am the way, the truth, and the life: no man cometh unto the Father, but by me."

Without the full armor of GOD, we are powerless, but if you have the "Full Armor of GOD" you will be able to face the enemy head on, and overcome him at every level he strikes from, as taught in:

- 2 Corinthians 2:11

"Lest Satan should get an advantage of us: for we are not ignorant of his devices."

I humbly hope this chapter expressed and demonstrated a small vision into what it means to put on the full armor of GOD. I chose "small vision" purposely. Scripture holds the "full picture;" my hope is to guide you to Scripture, hoping you will read the written word of GOD for yourself.

In this book, I display a tiny fraction on what Scripture teaches us, but I feel like the ones I chose were matching today's society. But the written word of GOD is what I am humbly trying to guide you to. If I can get a few brother and sister souls to read the written word of GOD and acquire wisdom and understanding in its teachings, the purpose of this book will be accomplished.

Seek GOD with all your heart and soul.

Chapter 15

Speaking the truth

-Telling the Truth-

The latter part of the verse – Psalm 15:2 says, "And speaketh the truth in his heart." Have you ever spoken a lie before? Are you were you haunted by the truth, and became restless? You became restless; you had to tell the truth before you had peace!

If you've ever felt that tingling sensation of mild discomfort, it's the Holy Spirit nudging you forward. The Blessed Holy Spirit is also called "The Spirit of Truth" according to – John 16:13 "Howbeit when he, the Spirit of truth, is come, he will guide you into all truth: for he shall not speak of himself; but whatsoever he shall hear, *that* shall he speak: and he will shew you things to come," and a person filled with The Holy Spirit will exhibit truth, which is one major characteristic of The Holy Spirit.

If you see someone who has become a perpetual liar and claims he has the Holy Spirit, then the person is deceiving himself and you. The Holy Spirit and lies are akin to light and darkness; nobody begs darkness to leave at the sight of light, where there is light, darkness evaporates.

The Spirit of GOD teaches us the truth of the scriptures, and makes us hold on to that which is the revelation of knowledge, the will of The Father.

Even if you were faced with the temptation of sin, where telling a lie is the best thing to do for you to get out of an awkward situation, you still won't do it. Not necessarily because of you, but by the Spirit of truth that abides in you.

Those in whom the Holy Spirit dwells will live a life of integrity, honesty, and uprightness. They will seek to tell the truth in whatever situation they are in knowing very well the consequences lying carries.

I demonstrated earlier in the book how the devil is the father of all lies, {John 8:44} and we are clearly taught in Scripture we cannot serve two masters at once, clearly explained in:

- Matthew 6:19-24

> 19 "Lay not up for yourselves treasures upon earth, where moth and rust doth corrupt, and where thieves break through and steal:"
>
> 20 "But lay up for yourselves treasures in heaven, where neither moth nor rust doth corrupt, and where thieves do not break through nor steal:"
>
> 21 "For where your treasure is, there will your heart be also."
>
> 22 "The light of the body is the eye: if therefore thine eye be single, thy whole body shall be full of light."
>
> 23 "But if thine eye be evil, thy whole body shall be full of darkness. If therefore the light that is in thee be darkness, how great is that darkness!"
>
> 24 "No man can serve two masters: for either he will hate the one, and love the other; or else he will hold to the one, and despise the other. Ye cannot* serve God and mammon."

"Mammon" is a biblical term for *riches*, often used to describe the debasing influence of material wealth. The term was used by Jesus in his famous Sermon on the Mount and also appears in The Gospel, according to Luke.

Scripture teaches us the importance of speaking truth, more accurately "truth in love." Here are a few examples of many verses I could have chosen to make my point, but in my humble opinion and hope, these select few should demonstrate the importance of speaking the truth.

John 4:24

> "God is a Spirit: and they that worship him must worship him in spirit and in truth."

Ephesians 4:14, 25

14 "That we *henceforth* be no more children, tossed to and fro, and carried about with every wind of doctrine, by the sleight of men, *and* cunning craftiness, whereby they lie in wait to deceive;"

15 "But speaking the truth in love, may grow up into him in all things, which is the head, *even* Christ:"

16 "From whom the whole body fitly joined together and compacted by that which every joint supplieth, according to the effectual working in the measure of every part, maketh increase of the body unto the edifying of itself in love."

17 "This I say therefore, and testify in the Lord, that ye henceforth walk not as other Gentiles walk, in the vanity of their mind,"

18 "Having the understanding darkened, being alienated from the life of God through the ignorance that is in them, because of the blindness of their heart:"

19 "Who being past feeling have given themselves over unto lasciviousness, to work all uncleanness with greediness."

20 "But ye have not so learned Christ;"

21 "If so be that ye have heard him, and have been taught by him, as the truth is in Jesus:"

22 "That ye put off concerning the former conversation the old man, which is corrupt according to the deceitful lusts;"

23 "And be renewed in the spirit of your mind;"

24 "And that ye put on the new man, which after God is created in righteousness and true holiness."

25 "Wherefore putting away lying, speak every man truth with his neighbour: for we are members one of another."

Proverbs 6:12-23

12 "A naughty person, a wicked man, walketh with a forward mouth"

13 "He winketh with his eyes, he speaketh with his feet, he teacheth with his fingers;"

14 "Frowardness *is* in his heart, he deviseth mischief continually;

he soweth discord."

15 "Therefore shall his calamity come suddenly; suddenly shall he be broken without remedy."

16 "These six *things* doth the LORD hate: yea, seven *are* an abomination unto him:"

17 "A proud look, a lying tongue, and hands that shed innocent blood,"

18 "A heart that deviseth wicked imaginations, feet that be swift in running to mischief,"

19 "A false witness *that* speaketh lies, and he that soweth discord among brethren"

20 "My son, keep thy father's commandment, and forsake not the law of thy mother:"

21 "Bind them continually upon thine heart, *and* tie them about thy neck."

22 "When thou goest, it shall lead thee; when thou sleepest, it shall keep thee; and *when* thou awakest, it shall talk with thee."

23 "For the commandment *is* a lamp; and the law *is* light; and reproofs of instruction *are* the way of life:"

Proverbs 17:20

"He that hath a froward heart findeth no good: and he that hath a perverse tongue falleth into mischief."

James 1:26

"If any man among you seem to be religious, and bridleth not his tongue, but deceiveth his own heart, this man's religion is vain."

Matthew 12:34-37

34 "O generation of vipers, how can ye, being evil, speak good things? for out of the abundance of the heart the mouth speaketh."

35 "A good man out of the good treasure of the heart bringeth

forth good things: and an evil man out of the evil treasure bringeth forth evil things."

36 "But I say unto you, That every idle word that men shall speak, they shall give account thereof in the day of judgment."

37 "For by thy words thou shalt be justified, and by thy words thou shalt be condemned."

I humbly beg you to observe how Scripture, the moral compass to our way of conduct in our everyday lives, clearly defines in: - Matthew 12:36 "But I say unto you, that every idle word that men shall speak, they shall give account thereof in the Day of Judgment"

Every idle word, not some, not a few, not many, "every idle word." Understanding in depths the full impact of to the words we choose to speak, a humble follower and believer in Jesus Christ must use it for good, positive, truth, displayed as light in the world.

I for one love and fear Almighty GOD. I am just a humble soul of sinful nature, unworthy of the Kingdom of Heaven of GOD the Father and my LORD and Savior Jesus Christ.

I discovered in Scripture no one enters the Kingdom of Heaven except through our LORD and Savior Jesus Christ, but I also discovered there is a way in which I must conduct myself in all things. I am far from perfect, but in Jesus Christ I am redeemed and made perfect. To display my love, gratitude, and appreciation, I do my best daily to follow the path laid out for us by Jesus Christ our LORD and Savior. I am a humble man, far from perfect, but improving every day, I keep my eyes on Jesus Christ.

Understanding very well, one day, every idle word I speak will stand in my presence, good and bad, on judgment day. Fully understanding reality changes my perception on how I should speak, and be careful and wise on the words I decide to use in my everyday conversations with fellow brother and sister souls. I am still a work in progress, correcting myself when I fall short of the path of Jesus Christ. But one thing I know for certain is I love Jesus Christ my LORD and Savior. Even though I may stumble and fall, He will lift me back up and never let me go if my heart is focused on Him.

Chapter 16

What Is It That Grieves the Holy Spirit?

The truth is, it is sin. Sin grieves the Holy Spirit. The next question you may ask is, "What sins grieve the Holy Spirit?" A very naïve and easy response to that question would be that all sins grieve the Holy Spirit. The truth is, that is correct, but we don't want to operate in generality, we want to talk more about specifics. Let's look at one sin, which grieves the Holy Spirit, what is one of the names of the Blessed Holy Spirit referred to as the "Spirit of Truth" in:

- John 16:13

"Howbeit when he, the Spirit of truth, is come, he will guide you into all truth: for he shall not speak of himself; but whatsoever he shall hear, *that* shall he speak: and he will shew you things to come."

Jesus called Him the Spirit of Truth, and if He is, then one of the sins that would be grieving Him is lying.

-Ephesians 4:25 lists lying as one of the sins that grieve him: "Wherefore putting away lying, speak every man truth with his neighbor: for we are members one of another."

Have you told a lie today? Okay, maybe not a lie. How about a half truth? Maybe a false impression. The Bible tells us, that lies grieve the Holy Spirit; it doesn't matter what name you give it; GOD forbids all forms of lying because lying goes against the nature and the character of Almighty GOD; it disrespects Him. He is a GOD of Truth.

One example in the scriptures speaks of this:

- Titus 1:2 "In hope of eternal life, which God, that cannot lie, promised before the world began;"

GOD will never lie, because lying is totally inconsistent with His holy character. This can be learned in -1 John 2:21: "I have not written unto you because ye know not the truth, but because ye know it, and that no lie is of the truth."

When Apostle John says, "No lie is of the truth," it means lying can never bless truth or make a situation righteous. Lies are based on this false idea we can hide a wrong and protect ourselves from the consequences of truth, by ignoring the facts. When lying only makes a problem worse, then a genuine confession on the other hand, leads to forgiveness, and peace, returning us back to a more righteous path, and into the hands of a caring and wise GOD.

Psalms 31:5-6

> 5 "Into thine hand I commit my spirit: thou hast redeemed me, O LORD God of truth."
> 6 "I have hated them that regard lying vanities: but I trust in the LORD."

Even the "false prophet" Balaam understood that, which is taught in:
- Numbers 23:19

"God *is* not a man, that he should lie; neither the son of man, that he should repent: hath he said, and shall he not do *it*? or hath he spoken, and shall he not make it good?"

Lying perverts the Holy Trinity; all three members of the GOD head are linked with truth. Therefore, we can conclude truth is essential to being GOD.

In - 1 Samuel 15:29

"And also the Strength of Israel will not lie nor repent: for he *is* not a man, that he should repent.", we see this also in; – Ezekiel 24:14 "I the LORD have spoken *it*: it shall come to pass, and I will do *it*; I will not go back, neither will I spare, neither will I repent; according to thy ways, and according to thy doings, shall they judge thee, saith the Lord GOD."

The Holy Spirit is called the Spirit of Truth, taught once more in scriptures in: - John 15:26

"But when the Comforter is come, whom I will send unto you from the Father, *even* the Spirit of truth, which proceedeth from the Father, he shall testify of me."

Then we have a statement from -1 John 5:6

"This is he that came by water and blood, *even* Jesus Christ; not by water only, but by water and blood. And it is the Spirit that beareth witness, because the Spirit is truth."

In a similar fashion, Jesus Christ said in- John 14:6

"Jesus saith unto him, I am the way, the truth, and the life: no man cometh unto the Father, but by me."

We are children of GOD. Let us behave like Our Father, who is the GOD of Truth. Every time you tell a lie, the devil jumps up and says, "That is my child." Every time you tell the truth, GOD says, "That is my child; my children tell the truth." There is contention for ownership; you are either a child of the devil, or a child of The LORD GOD Almighty, and the wonderful thing is no one else decides whose child you are, except you.

Now I want to ask you a question. In the last seven days, at any point, could the devil jump up in your life and say, "That's my child,"? Okay, let me ask you another question. In the last thirty days, at any point, did the devil jump up and say, "That is my child,"?

The number one identity of the devil we all know is telling lies. Of course, we were told of the mission of the devil on earth in the New

Testament in:
- John 10:10
      "The thief cometh not, but for to steal, and to kill, and to destroy: I am come that they might have life, and that they might have *it* more abundantly."

His mission is to kill, steal, and destroy. Have you ever wondered how the devil is going to achieve all these missions? He has no other way but through lies and deceit. He used this same method on Eve, and it worked. The lie he told in the beginning affected the world. That is to let you know the strength that every lie carries.

The Holy Bible says the devil is a liar and the father of lies. Taught to us in:

– John 8:44
      "Ye are of *your* father the devil, and the lusts of your father ye will do. He was a murderer from the beginning, and abode not in the truth, because there is no truth in him. When he speaketh a lie, he speaketh of his own: for he is a liar, and the father of it." This one sin makes you more like the devil.

Jesus was speaking to some set of people in this verse of the Bible. They claimed to be children of GOD; they believed one could just bare the title "child of GOD" without having the qualities of a child of GOD. Jesus had to make it clear what they were. He called them "children of the devil" because they were filled with the identity of their father, the devil.
      Biology tells us about genetics and traits. The genetic formation of the offspring is from the parent; some habits are transferred through genetics, and some characteristics are through the genes of the parents past, to the current.
      This is exactly what Jesus was telling the people: they were liars, and the only one who has this identity is the devil. There are no shortcuts to this; there is no way to sweetened this. What Jesus was saying is clear: "If you are a liar, you are of the devil." So many people in this world have made lying to be a normal thing. Some will go to the

extent of bearing false witness against someone. Telling lies has become part of humanity, but Jesus is saying it is not right.

This is one of the most wonderful things about the Bible and our LORD Jesus Christ. The Bible tells you how it is, and doesn't fold. You don't have to be a liar; you gain nothing from it but adoption into the family of the devil. There are no excuses for telling lies.

Scripture reveals a list of things displeasing to GOD in:

- Proverbs 6:16-19

> 16 "These six *things* doth the LORD hate: yea, seven *are* an abomination unto him:"
> 17 "A proud look, a lying tongue, and hands that shed innocent blood"
> 18 "An heart that deviseth wicked imaginations, feet that be swift in running to mischief,"
> 19 "A false witness *that* speaketh lies, and he that soweth discord among brethren"

Why do you think GOD dislikes a lying tongue? Simply because it is the trait of the devil. Christians are fond of something we call "white lies;" it is a kind of lie told to save oneself or not to implicate another person, also called the "necessary lie." Whatever name you call it, whatever description you give it, GOD did not give types of lies. He did not give categories of lies. He called them lies. A lie will always be a lie.

Do you tell lies and claim to be a child of GOD? That is not the trait of GOD. That is never the identity of GOD. You have all it takes to withdraw yourself from the family of the devil. You should not be part of the children of the devil. Don't allow lies to push you into the pit of lies.

Chapter 17
Understanding the Spirit of Lust

I will start this chapter with a verse from:

- Galatians 5: 16-26

> 16 "This I say then, walk in the Spirit, and ye shall not fulfill the lust of the flesh."
>
> 17 "For the flesh lusteth against the Spirit, and the Spirit against the flesh: and these are contrary the one to the other: so that ye cannot do the things that ye would."
>
> 18 "But if ye be led of the Spirit, ye are not under the law."
>
> 19 "Now the works of the flesh are manifest, which are these; Adultery, fornication, uncleanness, lasciviousness,"
>
> 20 "Idolatry, witchcraft, hatred, variance, emulations, wrath, strife, seditions, heresies,"
>
> 21 "Envyings, murders, drunkenness, revellings, and such like: of which I tell you before, as I have also told you in time past, that they which do such things shall not inherit the kingdom of God."
>
> 22 "But the fruit of the Spirit is love, joy, peace, longsuffering, gentleness, goodness, faith,"
>
> 23 "Meekness, temperance: against such there is no law."
>
> 24 "And they that are Christ's have crucified the flesh with the affections and lusts."
>
> 25 "If we live in the Spirit, let us also walk in the Spirit."
>
> 26 "Let us not be desirous of vain glory, provoking one another, envying one another."

Very rarely do you find people talking about this subject because it is a very real struggle in the lives of every man and woman, and that is lust. This book is not to condemn you, shout at you, that you are a sinner, and you will be casted in the lake of fire.

I am writing this book to inform you, to teach you. What the devil does is try to make some topics taboo, and the more he does this, the more he makes people feel they are the only person who struggles with these things. But the truth is, you are not the only one who struggles with lust. Lust is a real problem. It is something you don't outgrow naturally. There are teens struggling with lust, and there are seniors struggling with lust. It is not something you can simply ignore and think will go away.

Chapter 18

Overcoming the spirit of lust!

The good news is, through Christ, we can overcome the spirit of lust. I will give you some literal and practical plans to overcome lust.

If we want to overcome lust, we need to be aware of what lust is. Lust is a unique spirit. Lust is something that can make a person make silly, stupid decisions. Lust can make someone commit life altering decisions for the sake of momentary pleasure. But before we go into details about the dangers of lust, and why every man and woman should fight it, we should first know what exactly lust is.

Lust is a selfish greed, an excessive wanting of something to gratify oneself, an intense sexual desire or appetite. Each time the word "lust" is used in the Bible, it is never used in positive context. Rather, it is always seen in a negative light, relating primarily, either on strong desire for sexual immorality, or idolatrous worship.

Lust has a great connection with covetousness and greed. Lust begins from the heart of people until it also reflects in their actions and characters. If the way we craved and lusted for the things of this world was the same way we craved for GOD and spiritual things, our lives would be much more aligned to the purposes of GOD.

Lust comes in all shapes and sizes. Broadly speaking, lust does not only have to do with sexual gratification. People lust for money, for instance:

- 1Timothy 6: 9-10

> 9 "But they that will be rich fall into temptation and a snare, and *into* many foolish and hurtful lusts, which drown men in destruction and perdition"
>
> 10 "For the love of money is the root of all evil: which while some coveted after, they have erred from the faith, and pierced themselves through with many sorrows"

The scripture says those who want to be rich at all cost, will fall into temptation through their foolishness and hurtful lusts. Lust leads to destruction, both physically and spiritually. The love of money is the root of all evil. The word "love" in that passage in Greek means "a lustful kind of love." Lust in Greek is rendered as "epithumia" which means "a longing, especially for what is forbidden."

Eve had lust for the tree of knowledge of good and evil, even when she knew it was forbidden. Lust would not allow her to abstain from it, and since Eve failed to deal with lust, the entire world lost its position with GOD and became spiritually depraved. There is nothing good about lust; lust destroys.

We can conclude that all forms of lust lead to destruction. But we are going to focus on lust in a sexual content. There are three categories of lust the Bible enumerates: The lust of the eyes, the lust of the flesh, and the pride of life. If you cannot discipline your eyes, as a man or woman, if you cannot discipline the way you look at opposite sex, then you will be a victim of "the lust of the eyes."

Job made a covenant with his eyes, never to look at the nakedness of a maiden.

Job 31:1

"I made a covenant with mine eyes; why then should I think upon a maid?"

We all know we can't go through our lives with our eyes closed; it's not practical. There is a difference between just walking and someone catching your eyes; you don't have to stay there; you don't have to keep looking, move on with your day. Why do you need to look for a second time, or third time, or a prolonged period? The trick is "don't look;" so that is the first practical step; it's simply "don't look."

I think we can all agree there are different types of looking. When you are driving, or walking, or going about your business, you are looking, but there is a completely different type of looking when you are lusting over a person. That is what I am saying: "do not do" you know the type of looking that has you playing different scenarios in your mind.

Let's say you are walking down the street and see an attractive person; carry on with your business. You don't have to turn your head and start fantasizing; just "don't look." Every fornication started with someone looking; all adultery started with someone looking. It only takes you looking and lusting. That is the door the devil needs; that is the door the spirit of lust needs that "look." The Bible instructs us in:

- Ephesians 4:27:
"Neither give place to the devil."
David could not look away when he saw Bathsheba bathing on the rooftop;

- 2 Samuel 11:1-2:
1 "And it came to pass, after the year was expired, at the time when kings go forth to battle, that David sent Joab, and his servants with him, and all Israel; and they destroyed the children of Ammon, and besieged Rabbah. But David tarried still at Jerusalem."
2 "And it came to pass in an evening tide, that David arose from off his bed, and walked upon the roof of the king's house: and from the roof he saw a woman washing herself; and the woman *was* very beautiful to look upon."

This lust led him to commit adultery and murder, which brought a great consequence upon his life. It all started with him looking. This is my point about lust making people make bad decisions. David stole another man's wife, and then got that woman's husband killed because he got that man's wife pregnant.

2 Samuel 11:3-5

> 3 "And David sent and inquired after the woman. And one said, Is not this Bathsheba, the daughter of Eliam, the wife of Uriah the Hittite?"
>
> 4 "And David sent messengers, and took her; and she came in unto him, and he lay with her; for she was purified from her uncleanness: and she returned unto her house."
>
> 5 "And the woman conceived, and sent and told David, and said, I am with child."

The reason why lust is so dangerous is because it makes people make decisions they regret, that they know are bad. We all know, and I'm sure David also knew, that messing with another man's wife was never going to end well. Yet he still did it. Why? Because lust makes people act silly.

People destroy beautiful marriages for the sake of lust. People marry people they shouldn't marry because of lust. I know I am not writing lies. The person you marry is the most important decision a person will make, aside from giving their life to Christ. But that spirit of lust will make them marry the wrong person. Lust will make people spend money they should not be spending.

Now, let me ask you, has lust ever caused you to make silly decisions? Everything that happened to David started because he was looking. My first piece of practical advice is "don't look." Read it again: "don't look." One more time: "don't look."

The second practical step to overcome lust is "stay busy" and do the things you are supposed to be doing. David was supposed to be on the frontline in battle with his men, but instead, he had free time, and if you want the devil to find you, have a lot of free time.

The third practical step is doing the things you are supposed to be doing. Go home to your wife, go home to your husband and spend time with your family. Instead of being out and about in the world in your free time, be with your family. Instead of being out and about, go work for The LORD. If you are trying to nurse lust in your heart, or are practicing sins, it will bring about a dire consequence you will never be able to cope with. If you allow the cravings of your flesh to lead you, if you want to give your body all the comfort and pleasures it demands, then you have the lust of the flesh. People, who answer to the invitation to fornicate, have the lust of the flesh.

The fourth practical step can be found in:

- Galatians 5:16-19

16 "This I say then, Walk in the Spirit, and ye shall not fulfill the lust of the flesh."

17 "For the flesh lusteth against the Spirit, and the Spirit against the flesh: and these are contrary the one to the other: so that ye cannot do the things that ye would."

18 "But if ye be led of the Spirit, ye are not under the law."

19 "Now the works of the flesh are manifest, which are these; Adultery, fornication, uncleanness, lasciviousness,"

The only way to escape from lust is to walk in the Spirit. If you walk in the Spirit, you will never fulfill the lust of the flesh. The two are at variants.

Galatians 5:16 says:

"*This* I say then, Walk in the Spirit, and ye shall not fulfill the lust of the flesh."

Chapter 19

Marriage and becoming one!

Marriage, vows, and unions of two souls into one, this will be the focus of this chapter. My goal here is not to determine what is right by the ways of men, but what GOD our Father intended marriage to be. Unfortunately, we tend to assume the "Word of GOD" is outdated, old fashion, and should be manipulated to fit into our ways of life; we try to align The LORD's ways to better fit our ways. We define what is right or wrong, what is good and bad, what is acceptable and what is not.

Doesn't that sound familiar to you? Deciding the knowledge of good and evil! This correlates with "eating from the Tree of Knowledge of Good and Evil," don't you think? I will dedicate a chapter to this specific subject to give you my humble point of view of what "eating from the Tree of Knowledge of Good and Evil" means to me based on my understanding. But this chapter is about marriage, so let's get into it.

Scripture is specific on this subject; the ways we are to keep in this manner are quite clear how marriage should remain sacred and good. We see this taught in:

- Matthew 19:4-6

4 "And he answered and said unto them, Have ye not read, that he which made *them* at the beginning made them male and female,"

5 "And said, for this cause shall a man leave father and mother, and shall cleave to his wife: and they twain shall be one flesh?"

6 "Wherefore they are no more twain, but one flesh. What therefore God hath joined together, let not man put asunder."

Adultery is the only reason in the eyes of GOD our Father that would allow a person to divorce in accordance to His laws and teachings. The Pharisees questioned Jesus Christ on this subject, taught in:

- Matthew 19:7-9

> 7 "They say unto him, why did Moses then command to give a writing of divorcement, and to put her away?"
> 8 "He saith unto them, Moses because of the hardness of your hearts suffered you to put away your wives: but from the beginning it was not so."
> 9 "And I say unto you, Whosoever shall put away his wife, except *it be* for fornication, and shall marry another, committeth adultery: and whoso marrieth her which is put away doth commit adultery."

These teachings were spoken by Christ Himself, the ways of The LORD were true in the beginning of His creation stand true today, and will stand always. We tend to twist and mold scripture and the laws and ways to better fit our perception of evolution or so-called progress. We tend to choose the parts we like and ignore the parts we find more difficult to follow. That sounds to correlate with "lukewarm" believers, don't you think?

When I got married, there was one thing I clearly understood in the process of marriage. I was joining my soul with the woman I chose to be the mother of my children. Marriage is seen as blessed in the eyes of our Heavenly Father and should be undertaken with understanding and discernment of what marriage and vows truly mean.

Upon pronouncing my vows to the woman I love, standing before family and friends, and a pastor who proceeded our ceremony of marriage, I knew it wasn't just a promise to my wife-to-be; above all, it was me standing before Almighty GOD as my witness, giving my word and promise to Him, a promise I understood was made to my wife-to-be in the presence and blessing of GOD The Father. My vows held weight in the eyes of The LORD.

Above all, The LORD is the one I wish to please and obey, and

His ways are the ways I choose to follow. Once you understand marriage and vows are not only for your spouse, but are a commitment to The LORD, it might change your perspective on marriage. If, like me, your desire is to obey and follow in the ways of our LORD and Savior Jesus Christ, you might want to pay attention to what Scripture teaches and follow it.

Earlier, I spoke of becoming one is the process of marriage; I will establish what I meant with Scripture once again. As always, Scripture holds the answer. We saw earlier in:

- Matthew 19:5

"And said, for this cause shall a man leave father and mother, and shall cleave to his wife: and they twain shall be one flesh?"

But then if we look at:

- 1 Corinthians 6:15-20

15 "Do you not know that your bodies are members of Christ? Shall I then take the members of Christ and make them members of a prostitute? Never!"

16 "Or do you not know that he who is joined to a prostitute becomes one body with her? For, as it is written, the two will become one flesh."

17 "But he who is joined to the Lord becomes one spirit with him."

18 "Flee from sexual immorality. Every other sin a person commits is outside the body, but the sexually immoral person sins against his own body."

19 "Or do you not know that your body is a temple of the Holy Spirit within you, whom you have from God? You are not your own,"

20 "for you were bought with a price. So glorify God in your body."

Taking into account that sexual intercourse is to be kept in the confines of marriage, between a man and a woman, keeping the unity of marriage clean in the eyes of The LORD, clearly taught to us in:

- Hebrews 13:4

"Marriage *is* honorable in all, and the bed undefiled: but whoremongers and adulterers God will judge."

My humble opinion on the subject is marriage is a commitment to The LORD, of faithfulness to our spouse we declare to love, love him or her alone, and remain faithful to the marriage and the vows we have spoken, with the understanding the vows were not simply for your spouse and the wedding gathering, but in the presence and with the blessing of Almighty GOD.

Sexual intercourse is where the unifying of souls happens, as mentioned earlier in the book. We are spirits, with souls in a body of flesh having an earthly journey or adventure, depending on how you perceive it. Imagine it this way, if you will: sexual intercourse is the mixing of body fluids. As an example, I will use colors of juices to represent body fluids mixing together. The body is the material—the physical, the outer person. Now, let me demonstrate what happens in the body when you unite by sexual intercourse.

First, the sex organs unite as well as the bodies by mixing their fluids, the same way a glass of red juice mixes with another of yellow juice to give a mixture: an orange juice.

From one body to the other, fluids mix and unify the bodies of the two persons to become one flesh. Thus, you find the bodily fluids in one person are the same body fluids in his/her sex partner.

This is the reason diseases like gonorrhea, syphilis; HIV/AIDs, etc. are transmitted in sex. Much more, demons are also transmitted in sex. Many people do not understand that in sex you are unifying (mixing) your body with the other person's and if that other person has a disease, a demon, you already have it.

Now, let's examine what happens to the soul when you unite by sexual intercourse. Two souls unify to become one soul.

It is only in sex you find two people thinking and feeling the same. Ever wonder why couples fighting become happy after sex? Because the two have unified their souls (feelings, thinking, emotions, will, etc.) to be in the same wavelength.

Two people with one soul are referred to as "soulmates" because they have mated, mixed, or unified their souls to form one.

The spirit is no different. There is also a uniting of spirits which occurs when you have sexual intercourse with another person. A person's spirit is either connected to God's spirit (Holy Spirit) or to Satan's spirit (the evil spirit). Human's spirit does not live in a void, and there is nothing like being lukewarm, neither in God's camp nor Satan camp. You are either in one of the two, but you cannot be in both at the same time.

If one person is connecting her/his spirit with the Holy Spirit, and the other person is connecting her/his spirit with the Holy Spirit, the two spirits will unify easily in sex, forming one spirit. If one person's spirit is connected with the evil spirit and the other person's spirit too, the spirits will unify easily, forming one spirit. But when one person's spirit is connected with the Holy Spirit, and the other person's is connected with the evil spirit, the two spirits will repel each other and never unify.

If you asked God for a partner and see someone who is not a Christian coming to you, run away because that is not God's but Satan's. God only brings you a partner with the same spirit as you.

No matter how hard two people with different spirits try to unify with each other, they never become one flesh. The two spirits (Holy Spirit and evil spirit) repel and fight. Reason a marriage between a Christian and non-Christian is doomed from the start and never survives except when the Christian falls or the non-Christian changes her/his heart.

You can unify your bodies and souls, but the spirits, if different, cannot be unified, thus you will never be one flesh no matter how hard you try. In sex, you are unifying two temples of God to form one temple reason sex is a mystery. Sex is a Trinitarian relationship of God, self, and spouse. It is supernatural and divine, and must be kept in the confines of marriage in the eyes of The LORD.

Here are four examples how the world nowadays lies about sexual intercourse and the effects it has on your body, soul, and spirit:

- The world tells you that sex is just a bodily act which is a lie. Sex involves the body, the soul, and the spirit.
- The world tells you that you are an animal, thus you can have sex with every and any person which is a lie. You are created in an image and likeness of God while animals are not.
- The world tells you that God didn't create you but you evolved which is a lie. God created you.
- The world tells you that you can marry any person as long as you agree which is a lie. Yes! You will agree with your mouths, but if you have different spirits, your relationship is doomed.

What it means to become one can be defined as such. All the problems, spiritual problems of that person have become yours. If demons are attacking the other person, if there are spiritual attacks against the other person, it means there is also a door for these spirits to enter your life.

Society today has distorted and deceived many on the true meaning and purpose of marriage. If you truly love GOD the Father and wish to obey and live according to His will, you must read and study the written word of GOD in Scripture to acquire wisdom and understanding on the sanctity of marriage, and the manner in which we are to conduct ourselves in order to be righteous in the eyes of our Heavenly Father.

Simply declaring something is special has little to no meaning. To justify your words, one must truly believe it is special and act in accordance to the fact it is special with your actions and intentions, proving your belief it is be special. This principle is also relevant with one's claim to love someone. Simply speaking the words holds little to no impact; your actions and intentions prove the value you choose to give it.

Chapter 20

Not All Sins Are the Same
Sexual Immorality, Adultery, Fornication!

Several people share their body with many then wonder of all the misfortunes which befall them. Not all sins are the same, and here is what I mean by that. When you steal, you are not joining yourself to another person. When you lie, you are not joining yourself with another person. But if you have sexual intercourse, you are joining yourself to someone and opening doors in your life.

You may look at sexual immorality, adultery, and fornication as a sin you can just commit and ask for forgiveness. The scar that such actions will leave on your body, soul, and spirit, even after you ask for forgiveness, will be huge and follow you a very long time. Many people are still battling with the scar that sexual immorality, adultery, and fornication has or had on them.

Why do you think break-ups are so painful? You haven't spoken to that person for years, but you still feel connected to them. You are still daydreaming about that person. You are joined to that person.

Don't destroy your body; don't destroy yourself due to pleasure. Don't send GOD away from your body because of sexual immorality. Holiness is important. Let anyone call you anything they want to persuade you of such things. Deep down inside, they wish they could be like you.

Never let the pleasure of flesh make you destroy yourself. Flee sexual immorality, don't stay around it, don't pursue it, and never give in to temptations sent by the evil one. We are taught this in scripture, clearly explained in:

- 1 Corinthians 10:12-13

> 12 "Wherefore let him that thinketh he standeth take heed lest he fall."
>
> 13 "There hath no temptation taken you but such as is common to man: but God *is* faithful, who will not suffer you to be tempted above that ye are able; but will with the temptation also make a way to escape, that ye may be able to bear *it*."

It is a wildfire you should never play with. It spreads and consumes anything in its path. If you allow this in you, it will spread and consume you. Sexual immorality is not limited to fornication, it is found in adultery as well.

For anyone who is not married, purity is important. GOD wants you to be. GOD wants you to keep yourself pure, because you are carrying Him in you. We are taught this in:

- 1 Corinthians 6:19

"What? Know ye not that your body is the temple of the Holy Ghost *which is* in you, which ye have of God, and ye are not your own?"

Don't let anyone deceive you into doing what is wrong. They will say many things to you, but don't ever become part of them. Sexual immorality is a sin. The Bible called it a sin. It can destroy your life, and sexual immorality will send you to hell. We are taught this in:

- Hebrews 13:4

"Marriage *is* honorable in all, and the bed undefiled: but whoremongers and adulterers God will judge."

GOD will surely judge everyone who commits this sin. It doesn't matter what repercussions this sin brings physically, it doesn't matter the scar it will give anyone who commits it. The main thing is it is a sin, and GOD will judge those who are committing it. Do you want GOD to judge you? Do you want the wrath of GOD to fall upon you? I sure don't, but that's me.

You need to run from these sins, you need to abstain. Don't let the devil get you to slip into these sins. I know the temptation will always come; the devil will always send temptation in your way to make you fall. You can overcome the temptation; you can come out victorious. Scripture teaches us in:

- James 4:7

"Submit yourselves therefore to God. Resist the devil, and he will flee from you."

The devil wants to destroy your marriage, your family, your holiness. But above all, the devil wants to get you to sin in away way he can. The devil understands very well when you sin, you are separated from the presence of GOD the Father, making you easy prey for his schemes to enslave you even more in sin, hoping to turn you away from Jesus Christ. But if you resist the devil, he will flee from you.

The evil one will try to break the sanctity of your marriage with temptations, lies, and deceit. He will send opportunities and occasions to sin, he will whisper in your ears that nobody will know, nobody will be hurt, that the consequences are worth the risk, that you are doing nothing wrong. But trust me, if you truly believe in the word of GOD and the teachings of Scripture, you know that is false, a deception from the deceiver, spoken from the father of all lies who likes to twist Scripture to make you believe in his lies.

-1 Corinthians 7:2

"Nevertheless, *to avoid* fornication, let every man have his own wife, and let every woman have her own husband."

Sexual intercourse is to be kept in the confines of marriage, between a man and a woman, for purpose of procreation, to satisfy our sexual desires, and resist the temptation to give in to sexual immorality.

Chapter 21

Facing the Last Days Without Fear

How can I overcome my fear of the end of days? How do I overcome the spirit of fear that stops me from pursuing GOD's purpose intended for me in my life? The Bible tells us how in:

- 2 Timothy 1:7

"For God hath not given us the spirit of fear; but of power, and of love, and of a sound mind."

Fear is not of GOD; rather, it is one of the most efficient weapons in the hand of the devil to war against the heart of believers. In fact, the Bible says fear is a spirit; it makes people feel defeated, even before the day of battle. So, the devil will always attempt to captivate our hearts with fear, knowing anyone who fears is held captive by whatsoever he or she fears.

Job said the things he feared had happened to him. That means we are most likely to fall victim of what we fear. But we can never be afraid of what we know. Heaven is our home. Our full assurance of this will deal with fear in our hearts. In order to counter the operation of spirit of fear in our hearts, GOD gave us the Spirit of Power, Spirit of Love, and a sound mind.

With these, we can conquer fear all the way. Do the signs of the end time make you scared? Are you instilled with fearful emotions? Each time you hear about the wars, earthquakes, famines, natural disasters, great tribulation, the seven bowls of GOD's wrath, and the likes, which are to characterize the last days?

Ignorance, coupled with a wrong belief system, can result in confusion and unnecessary anxiety about the end time. The Bible has told us what will happen in the last days, not because GOD wants us to fear the events, but so we might be assured of our victory after all is set and done. The information given in scriptures about the last days is to guide and help us to prepare.

Not to be left behind in GOD's agenda for the church of Christ. So it is necessary for us to be informed. However, we must not be bound to fear, we are taught in:

- John 16:33

"These things I have spoken unto you, that in me ye might have peace. In the world ye shall have tribulation: but be of good cheer; I have overcome the world."

If we keep walking in Christ, our victory is predetermined, and there is no cause for fear. We are not fighting for victory; rather, we are fighting in victory. We are fighting from a place and position of victory. Here are some things you need to know and do in order to overcome the fear of the last days. One, repent of your fear, fear is evil. We see this in:

- Revelations 21:8

"But the fearful, and unbelieving, and the abominable, and murderers, and whoremongers, and sorcerers, and idolaters, and all liars, shall have their part in the lake which burneth with fire and brimstone: which is the second death."

This verse includes the fearful and unbelieving as part of those who will not make it to Heaven. We need to repent of our fear, because it shows we do not trust GOD enough. We must repent, first, from our fears of the end time and trust in the power of Christ which is able to save us to the uttermost; fear binds; it is self-imprisonment.

You can imagine what would happen to those who are subject to fear for their lifetime when they get to Heaven and discover what they feared was not real. If we can overcome fear, we can overcome the devil. Listen, the devil isn't as powerful as most of us think; he only uses fear to defeat people before their actual defeat.

The devil can't stop you from going to Heaven, but he knows if he can inject you with fear, he can make your life, whilst you are still here on earth, a living hell. He knows once you are on Heaven, he can't get to you, but he is determined to make your life here on earth miserable, and does this by pushing you towards fear.

We all need to repent of fear and ask GOD for strength and boldness to walk with Him. Ask GOD to forgive you for giving room to fear and not trusting Him enough. In the Bible we are taught in:

Psalm 23:1-6:

> 1 "{A Psalm of David.} The LORD *is* my shepherd; I shall not want"
>
> 2 "He maketh me to lie down in green pastures: he leadeth me beside the still waters."
>
> 3 "He restoreth my soul: he leadeth me in the paths of righteousness for his name's sake."
>
> 4 "Yea, though I walk through the valley of the shadow of death, I will fear no evil: for thou *art* with me; thy rod and thy staff they comfort me."
>
> 5 "Thou preparest a table before me in the presence of mine enemies: thou anointest my head with oil; my cup runneth over."
>
> 6 "Surely goodness and mercy shall follow me all the days of my life: and I will dwell in the house of the LORD forever."

Another example is - 2 Timothy 1:7

"For God hath not given us the spirit of fear; but of power, and of love, and of a sound mind."

Each time you are confronted with the spirit of fear, always remember the fourth verse of - Psalm 23: "Yea, though I walk through the valley of the shadow of death, I will fear no evil: for thou *art* with me; thy rod and thy staff they comfort me". When uttering such words in the Spirit, they must hold conviction and authority in the name of Christ.

Do not utter such words with doubt. If you are a true believer and follower of Our LORD and Savior Jesus Christ, you must utter such words with faith and belief, understanding very well that in the name of Jesus Christ our Lord, stands all power and authority, forever and ever.

Second, you need to comfort yourself with the scriptures:

-Romans 15:4 say: "For whatsoever things were written aforetime were written for our learning, that we through patience and comfort of the scriptures might have hope."

All the prophecies recorded in the Bible about the end time and all the events that will characterize it, were written for our learning. GOD would not have us ignorant about his plans; therefore, as he reveals them to His prophets; they put them into records, so the council of GOD might be passed from one generation to the other.

The purpose for documenting the last days' events is not to instill fear in us; they were written for our learning, you see. Nothing instills fear more than ignorance; when you do not know a thing, you will be afraid of it. Fear of the unknown has caused havoc in people's lives. The signs of the end time, which are now being fulfilled, are not surprising to us, because the scriptures have prepared our minds for them.

The world may be confused, but in the written "Word of GOD," we get inside information, we discern with knowledge given by The Holy Spirit, we rule by knowledge. We do not just know what is presently, we are also aware of that which is to come. The ultimate reason the prophecies of the end times were recorded for our learning is we might patiently wait for its fulfillment, and find comfort through the scriptures which recorded them.

We know for an instance the rapture in nearer than ever before; we know this because of the events going on in the world right now. So, we can be comforted that soon we will be taken out of this evil world, and if Christ lingers to return, we would patiently wait for the fulfillment of the promise. The scripture is what fuels the hope of believers, many of the things recorded in the times past have been ful-filled, while some are being fulfilled.

This gives us hope, that others will be fulfilled, so we are not hopeless. We can always comfort ourselves through the scriptures, knowing GOD has ordained a better promise for us, to whom the end of the world is coming.

Thirdly, establish a working relationship with the Holy Spirit, to overcome this fear of the end time. Every believer must reignite their passion for The Holy Spirit and establish a working daily relationship with him.

We can only receive such power after The Holy Spirit has come upon us. He must not just inhabit us once, but he must also remain within us always.

As believers of the end time, we need The Holy Spirit every minute, and for as long as there is breathe in our lungs and a pulse to our heart. The Holy Spirit produces the fruit of love, a measure against the spirit of fear. You cannot have a working relationship with the Holy Spirit, and be afraid of the end time, or the events of the end time.

The Holy Spirit is our comforter, helper, strengthener, and standby. He will help us all the way; it is dangerous for you to journey without the Holy Spirit at such a time as this. He is our "Great Companion." He strengthens our faith when we are weak, He gives us boldness in hard times, and he helps us at crucial times of need.

Loneliness is one of the causes of fear, but we are not alone; the Holy Spirit is with you, so there is no cause to fear. Only walk consistently with the Holy Spirit. There is a great and unexplained joy the Holy Spirit produces in the hearts of those who walk with Him. You can't have that joy and still nurture fear in your heart.

Fourthly, realize you are chosen, and beloved by GOD. We can see an example of this in:

- 1 Peter 2:9-

"But ye *are* a chosen generation, a royal priesthood, an holy nation, a peculiar people; that ye should shew forth the praises of him who hath called you out of darkness into his marvelous light"

We mean more to GOD than our hearts can ever conceive. We didn't choose GOD first, He was the one who chose and made us who we are, and a particular people to Himself. GOD called us out of the darkness that He might bring us into His marvelous light. He rescued us from the world, into His Kingdom, His Glorious Kingdom.

Your fear about the end time will come to an end the moment you realize GOD chose you by Himself, and you are the apple of His eyes.

GOD did not choose us to destroy us, He chose us that we might be saved and live with Him throughout all eternity. What are you worried about? Remember GOD is in control. 1 John 4:18-19 says something very powerful about the relationship between the love of GOD for us and fear.

1 John 4:18-19
> 18 "There is no fear in love; but perfect love casteth out fear: because fear hath torment. He that feareth is not made perfect in love."
> 19 "We love him, because he first loved us."

We cannot measure the length, and the breath, and the heights, and the depths of GOD's love for us. Beloved, there is nothing more powerful in all existence than the perfect love of GOD. See how in the same way GOD willingly delivered up Jesus for you. He is right now, more than willing to heal you, protect you, provide for you, and give you good success today, because you are GOD's beloved, nothing can ever separate you from His presence, His favor, His love, and His help.

We don't need to fear what would become of us at the end time if we are in Christ. The fear of the end time is not for us. We are the beloved of GOD, and His love cast out all fear. He who fears is not yet made perfect in the love of GOD. The Love of GOD cannot coexist with fear in our hearts, all you need to do in this end time, is to remind yourself of the love of GOD, and your fears will give way.

The only time we are told to fear is in GOD. We can see this in:

- Psalm 111:10

"The fear of the LORD *is* the beginning of wisdom: a good understanding have all they that do *his commandments*: his praise endureth forever"

We can also see it taught to us in:

- Proverbs 24:21

"My son, fear thou the LORD and the king: *and* meddle not with them that are given to change."

Many more examples are in the scriptures, but I will stick to these two for now. No other time are we told in the Bible to fear, except to fear GOD Himself. If you truly fear The LORD, you will obey his teachings and commandments.

Chapter 22
Conclusion of the Book

Fire is just a Test that Will Refine You to Become Pure

Proverbs 3:5-6

> 5 "Trust in the LORD with all thine heart; and lean not unto thine own understanding."
>
> 6 "In all thy ways acknowledge him, and he shall direct thy paths."

If you trust GOD, you will become stronger irrespective of the test you go through, or you will go through.

Hard times are just a test, and have a purpose to those who love our LORD and Savior Jesus Christ.

Faith improves with test or trials in our lives:

- John 16:33

> "These things I have spoken unto you, that in me ye might have peace. In the world ye shall have tribulation: but be of good cheer; I have overcome the world."

Jesus Christ taught us these things in the Holy Bible; He knew we were going to face trials and tests.

You may be going through tribulations today, but if you walk through it with belief and trust in Jesus Christ as your LORD and Savior, although you might be going through fire today, you will come out of it as pure as gold.

Is there anything GOD our Heavenly Father cannot do?

If you know who Jesus Christ our LORD and Saviour truly is, you will never doubt Him, even in the toughest times of your life here on earth.

Don't you know the LORD sees the test you are facing? Do you think our LORD and Saviour Jesus Christ don't care?

He knows, He sees, He cares, and He will stand beside you, and guide you, and protect you, and empower you to overcome any test and tribulation sent your way.

-Isaiah 43:2

"When thou passest through the waters, I *will be* with thee; and through the rivers, they shall not overflow thee: when thou walkest through the fire, thou shalt not be burned; neither shall the flame kindle upon thee."

When you walk through fire you shall not be burnt.

They want us divided, unable to gather, they don't want us to have the opportunity to share faith in Jesus because it is the truth. As mentioned before, taught to us in:

- John 14:6

"Jesus saith unto him, I am the way, the truth, and the life: no man cometh unto the Father, but by me."

We are all humans, we are all on this earth created by GOD, and GOD wants us to share the truth with everyone, and at every opportunity that we have.

Sometimes, the only Bible that anybody will ever read is just us. They will read us, they will never pick up the Scripture and read them word for word, but they will see in our actions,

We are walking letters of GOD, guided by the written words of GOD the Father, taught to us in Scripture, exemplified by Jesus Christ, His only Son, and our LORD and Saviour, who by His purpose, took upon Himself the sins of the whole world, which was and still is our new covenant with GOD the Father since the fall of mankind due to the actions of Adam and Eve.

Lucifer and one third of the angels fell and became known as the devil and his demons. The devil corrupted and deceived Adam and Eve in betraying Almighty GOD. Adam and Eve were created in the image of Almighty GOD; they were perfect, but after they disobeyed GOD the Father, they no longer represented the holiness of GOD the Father.

Disobedience made them unholy, unclean, unrighteous, and above all, unworthy of the Kingdom of Heaven. The fall of GOD's perfect creation took root in the Garden of Eden when Adam and Eve were deceived by the serpent, also known as the devil, to disobey GOD the Father; therefore, corrupting GOD's perfect creation.

No man is worthy of the Kingdom of Heaven, clearly taught in:

- Romans 3:23 26 -Righteousness through Faith-
>   23 "for all have sinned and fall short of the glory of God,"
>   24 "Being justified freely by his grace through the redemption that is in Christ Jesus:"
>   25 "Whom God hath set forth to be a propitiation through faith in his blood, to declare his righteousness for the remission of sins that are past, through the forbearance of God;"
>   26 "To declare, I say, at this time his righteousness: that he might be just, and the justifier of him which believeth in Jesus."

Jesus Christ our LORD and Savior, Son of Almighty GOD the Father, is the only one worthy of such a title. He is the only one righteous in the eyes of Almighty GOD. By the righteousness of Jesus Christ's life and purpose, we are saved.

Our LORD and Savior Jesus Christ exemplified the way in which we are to conduct ourselves in order to obey and be righteous in the eyes of The LORD. Jesus taught us the way in which we are to love each other, treat each other, care for each other, respect each other, and live with each other, as taught in:

- John 14:1-6
>   1 "Let not your heart be troubled: ye believe in God, believe also in me."

2 "In my Father's house are many mansions: if it were not so, I would have told you. I go to prepare a place for you."

3 "And if I go and prepare a place for you, I will come again, and receive you unto myself; that where I am, there ye may be also."

4 "And whither I go ye know, and the way ye know."

5 "Thomas saith unto him, Lord, we know not whither thou goest; and how can we know the way?"

6 "Jesus saith unto him, I am the way, the truth, and the life: no man cometh unto the Father, but by me."

I will conclude this book with a hopeful heart, praying it might guide someone to the written word of GOD, If you truly seek Jesus Christ, forgiveness, repentance, path of obedience, and righteousness, how to love and obey Almighty GOD, Scripture will give you wisdom and understanding, and clear directions to the path we must follow.

Use Scripture as a compass to remain on the right path, keep your focus on Jesus Christ our LORD and Savior, put on the "full armor of GOD," bear good fruits, pray, trust, hope, keep the faith, love unconditionally, and always put Almighty GOD first in all things you do.

Love Comes from God

1 John 4:7-21

7 "Beloved, let us love one another: for love is of God; and every one that loveth is born of God, and knoweth God."

8 "He that loveth not knoweth not God; for God is love."

9 "In this was manifested the love of God toward us, because that God sent his only begotten Son into the world, that we might live through him."

10 "Herein is love, not that we loved God, but that he loved us, and sent his Son *to be* the propitiation for our sins."

11 "Beloved, if God so loved us, we ought also to love one another."

12 "No man hath seen God at any time, if we love one another, God dwelleth in us, and his love is perfected in us."

13 "Hereby know we that we dwell in him, and he in us, be-

cause he hath given us of his Spirit."

14 "And we have seen and do testify that the Father sent the Son *to be* the Saviour of the world."

15 "Whosoever shall confess that Jesus is the Son of God, God dwelleth in him, and he in God."

16 "And we have known and believed the love that God hath to us. God is love; and he that dwelleth in love dwelleth in God and God in him."

17 "Herein is our love made perfect, that we may have boldness in the Day of Judgment: because as he is, so are we in this world."

18 "There is no fear in love; but perfect love casteth out fear: because fear hath torment. He that feareth is not made perfect in love."

19 "We love him, because he first loved us."

20 "If a man say, I love God, and hateth his brother, he is a liar: for he that loveth not his brother whom he hath seen, how can he love God whom he hath not seen?"

21 "And this commandment have we from him, that he who loveth God love his brother also."

Grace and Mercy to All

Special thanks to a great artist, Alexandra Brunet, for giving life to the book design. Great is your talent and greater is your potential.